SUCCESS WITH SIMULATION

A definitive guide to process improvement success using
simulation for healthcare, manufacturing, and warehousing

By

Hosni Adra

Success with Simulation

Success with Simulation

Hosni Adra
3909 75th St. Ste 103
Aurora, IL 60504

Ordering Information:
Quantity sales. Special discounts are available on quantity purchases by corporations, associations, and others. For details, contact the publisher at the address above.

Publisher's Cataloging-in-Publication data
Hosni Adra
Success with Simulation. A definitive guide to process improvement success using simulation for healthcare, manufacturing, and warehousing/Hosni Adra

ISBN 978-1-7329878-0-7

First Edition

Preface

This book is a culmination of many years of experience in the field of simulation and process improvement. Beginning in the early 90s, I was fascinated with simulation and its ability to mitigate risks and improve efficiency. Back then, simulation was hard to use, cumbersome to implement, and was not widely available.

My mission was to create a simulation environment that applies to all industries and can be used by anyone. I then created an interactive simulation environment that is both easy to use and highly efficient.

Throughout my journey I have applied the technology to many industries and a multitude of problems. By utilizing the developed solution I was able to understand the industry and help guide the creation of one of the most successful simulation tools today, Simcad Pro.

My experience with different industries helped me understand the issues they face and allowed me to bridge the gap in the technology among them. By applying tools from one industry to another I generated unique and effective solutions to complex problems.

Following the TQM and lean revolution, companies required lean methodology to be implemented. Yet, many saw the transition as too risky and different than the current way. Simulation was, and still is, the tool required to help in that transition by reducing the associated risk and proving to the skeptical that the transition is better than current status quo. Change is never easy, it is the natural transition to better things, but without change there is no progress.

During my journey, I have discussed simulation progress and advances with many colleagues with various degrees of simulation knowledge. Some stopped believing in the technology because of a failed project or a bad experience. Others didn't believe that a simulation model can be built fast enough to be useful. To my surprise, some educators were unwilling to change to newer technology due to the strain it puts on their curriculum.

My goal in writing this book is to help everyone with an interest in simulation to select the correct tool, identify the proper goals, and follow a step by step approach to success. Incorporating simulation in business decisions is a key to its success. This book also covers migrating simulation technology to utilize real-time data and provide real-time predictive and prescriptive analytics. This is the ultimate use of a mature and well understood simulation environment.

Dedication

I've been blessed with a beautiful family, amazing wife, kids and great co-workers, without whom this book wouldn't be possible. To my Wife, thank you for your love, patience and support to keep me on track. To my family, thank you for the support and feedback in getting my thoughts together. And, to my co-workers, the CreateASoft team, thank you for your feedback and help.

Success with Simulation

About the Author

HOSNI ADRA is the co-founder of CreateASoft, Inc., headquartered in Aurora IL. He has been involved in Process Improvement and Simulation for more than 25 years. Hosni has applied his process improvement expertise to multiple industries including healthcare, manufacturing and warehousing. As the holder of several patents in the fields of dynamic simulation, interactive simulation, and real-time tracking, Hosni has been a sought after expert in these fields and has presented multiple papers on process improvement using simulation and on implementing lean concepts. With his dedication to the use of technology to improve efficiency and output, he has positioned CreateASoft as a leader in the process improvement industry.

Table of Contents

Chapter 1: Introduction

WHAT IS A SIMULATION?

The Oxford Dictionary describes simulation as the "imitation of a situation or process."[1] Simulation by this definition has been around for thousands of years. The idea of replicating natural processes is the foundation of the scientific method. For example, anyone who has ever played a sport can attest to the importance of perfecting a technique in a practice environment before the time comes to use that skill.

The Merriam-Webster Dictionary's definition goes further, calling simulation the "examination of a problem often not subject to direct experimentation by means of a simulating device."[2] Simulation, then, might include anything from an online dissection in a seventh-grade biology class to a car crash test with a sensor-covered dummy in the driver's seat.

It is already clear that the concept of simulation can describe many different actions. According to the Institute for Simulation and Training at the University of Central Florida (UCF), "[in] its broadest sense, simulation is imitation.... Simulations (and models, too) are abstractions of reality."[3] This element is crucial:

---

[1] "Simulation," *Oxford Dictionaries*, accessed May 31, 2017, https://en.oxforddictionaries.com/definition/simulation.

[2] "Simulation," *Merriam-Webster Dictionary,* accessed May 31, 2017, https://www.merriam-webster.com/dictionary/simulation.

[3] "What is simulation?" *University of Central Florida Institute for Simulation and Training*, last modified July 1, 2014, http://www.ist.ucf.edu/background.htm.

a simulation involves the use of an abstraction or imitation so that the real subject is not to be harmed.

Keeping all of these facets of the definition in mind, simulation can be summarized as any system that is used to mimic reality in order to determine outcomes without disrupting the real-world environment.

Within this definition, the contexts in which one might use a simulation are limited only by one's imagination. The U.S. government, for example, has emphasized the importance of computer simulation as "an indispensable tool for resolving a multitude of scientific and technological problems facing our country."[4] The NSF has been an enthusiastic promoter of engineering simulations in particular through the establishment of a Blue Ribbon Panel in Simulation Based Engineering Science.

On the other side of the world, medical outpatient departments in Hong Kong use simulation modeling to manage patient congestion during busy times. Using the simulation, department managers can test different variables, such as consultation length and the use of an appointment system, in order to determine how to treat everyone in an efficient, satisfactory manner.[5]

---

[4] National Science Foundation Blue Ribbon Panel on Simulation-Based Engineering Science. "Simulation-Based Engineering Science: Revolutionizing Engineering Science through Simulation" (report, 2006, p. ix), https://www.nsf.gov/pubs/reports/sbes_final_report.pdf.

[5] L Aharonson-Daniel, RJ Paul, and AJ Hedley, "Management of queues in out-patient departments: the use of computer simulation." *Journal of Management in Medicine* 10, no. 6 (1996): 50-58. https://www.ncbi.nlm.nih.gov/pubmed/10538033

In both these places and everywhere in between, simulations make life easier and safer; for more people every day. They help businesses cut down on waste and do more with the resources they have. They also serve a vital role in education. Students have the opportunity to practice their skills in a low-risk environment—whether they intend to become doctors, soldiers, pilots, or any number of other professions.

Simulations can fall into a number of different categories. However, the primary two groups are human-driven simulations, which use actors, and computer-assisted simulations, which rely more heavily on technology.

HUMAN-DRIVEN SIMULATIONS

Human-driven simulations require three elements:

- a mockup of the environment to be simulated,
- actors to represent the items or persons to be simulated, and
- providers to perform the simulations.

Mockups of the environment are incredibly useful in the simulation process. They can be particularly helpful in considering equipment positioning in order to optimize efficiency, improve tools accessibility, and reduce repetitive stress.

For example, when designing operating rooms (OR), architectural firms use:

- life-like OR models,
- a complete staff as it exists in a real operating room, and
- a patient dummy to be operated on.

The actors (surgeons, nurses, anesthesiologists, and so on) interact with the patient and equipment in the simulated environment as they would with a real patient. This simulation helps to maximize space utilization,[1] improve equipment positioning for ease of access, and reduce unnecessary walking and travel within the operating room.

Using similar technology, manufacturers can also use mockup stations to improve their machinery design and minimize repetitive stress on their workers. In addition, these simulations can help to arrange a manufacturing setup such that all tools and resources are positioned within the worker's strike zone. This design eliminates unnecessary movement that may induce fatigue and reduce the worker's efficiency.

Along with environment mockups, actors play a crucial role in human-driven simulations. A common example of a human-driven simulation in which actors are prominent is a hospital disaster drill. Actors are given specific instructions about their role and hospital staff members are expected to treat them like real patients. These drills can help to identify weak points in the hospital's system, such as a staff shortage during certain busy times or long wait times for machine use.[6]

Simulations in the form of drills like these can also have unexpected benefits beyond weakness identification. Allowing invested personnel—for example, bio-design students or physicians—to participate in these drills as patient actors can

---

[6] Gofrit et al., "The efficacy of integrating 'smart simulated casualties' in hospital disaster drills." *Prehospital and Disaster Medicine* 12, no. 2 (1997): 97-101. https://www.ncbi.nlm.nih.gov/pubmed/10187010

help them to appreciate their role in a larger system as well as foster empathy for the real patients their work aims to help.[7]

The U.S. Federal Emergency Management Agency (FEMA) also relies on human-driven simulation to keep its staff prepared for emergencies of all kinds. By maintaining a cast of diverse and talented actors to take several different roles in emergency simulations, FEMA helps its employees to take drills seriously and to be prepared for complex and potentially dangerous circumstances.[8]

The use of actors in simulations has both benefits and drawbacks. It is advantageous to use actors rather than genuinely ill patients in hospital drills, for example, because actors can demonstrate more consistency in symptoms over multiple trials. Plus, healthy actors are not at risk of health complications if treatment does not go according to plan in an unusual scenario.[9]

Actors must be trained for their roles and paid for their involvement. This requires an input of time and money that may put financial strain on some institutions. In addition, even the most talented actors cannot always embody certain symptoms

---

[7] Stacey Paris Mccutcheon, "'Humbling' hospital simulations inspire Stanford graduate students to solve problems in health care delivery," *Stanford News* (Stanford, CA), May 10, 2017. http://news.stanford.edu/2017/05/10/hospital-simulations-inspire-student-innovators/.

[8] "Role Players Offer Real-World Training Experience," *Center for Domestic Preparedness,* accessed May 31, 2017, https://cdp.dhs.gov/news-media/article/role-players-offer-real-world-training-experience.

[9] "Using Standardized Patients in Teaching and Assessment," *University of Pittsburgh Office of Medical Education,* last modified August 4, 2016, http://www.omed.pitt.edu/standardized/teaching-benefit.php.

believably—for example, a heart murmur or high blood pressure.[10] These constraints can be mitigated depending on the details of the simulation (and the creativity of those running it!), but they are important considerations nonetheless.

The third element of human-driven simulation is the reaction of the providers. In the above examples, the physicians and FEMA staff members would be the providers. It is their job to react to the stimuli that the actors embody and treat the drill as if it were real. The providers' reaction to the actors becomes the outcome of the simulation exercise.

It is therefore the providers' reaction that determines the effectiveness of the human-driven simulation. If they respond well and their facilities are capable of managing the simulation's difficult conditions, there is little change necessary. If they are unable to cope with the challenges, they can identify problems encountered in the simulation that led to this failure and develop systems to prevent those issues from occurring in real life.

COMPUTER-ASSISTED SIMULATIONS

Computer-assisted simulations can have much in common with human-driven simulations. The key difference is that computer-assisted simulations are driven by technology rather than actors.

Computer-assisted simulations might involve virtual reality technology or 3D imaging. They may use animated graphics to

---

[10] JP Collins and RM Harden, "The Use of Real Patients, Simulated Patients and Simulators in Clinical Examinations," *Association for Medical Education in Europe*, AAME Medical Education Guide no. 13, https://web.archive.org/web/20071023055610/http://www.medev.ac.uk/resources/features/AMEE_summaries/Guide13summaryMay04.pdf.

help visualize a simulation. They may also crunch numbers and calculate probabilities quickly enough to predict events in the near future.

These simulations are already widely used. Some familiar examples are in weather forecasting, flight simulation, and online training exercises for students and new employees.[11] Computers have become an important part of everyday life. The simulations they are capable of running have revolutionized our ability to learn from historical data and use it to improve future endeavors.

Gaming is another facet of computer-assisted simulations. Tamagotchi pets, the popular Sims franchise, and first-person shooter games like Call of Duty are all examples of computerized programs. They are designed to imitate certain aspects of life— caring for a pet, fighting in combat, and so on—without introducing the real-life risks that engaging in such activities would pose. Such games are used for recreational purposes. Other simulation games can be used for career training purposes or other functions.

Computers have expanded the learning possibilities simulations can provide. One notable use of computer-assisted simulations was in former U.S. President Barack Obama's campaign against Republican candidate Mitt Romney. While Romney had a highly qualified team, Obama's campaign relied heavily on thousands of computer-assisted simulations to determine the best strategy.[12]

---

[11] "Computer Modeling and Simulation," National Institutes of Health Office of Management, accessed May 31, 2017, https://www.ors.od.nih.gov/OD/OQM/cms/Pages/default.aspx.

[12] Greg Satell, "Why the Future of Innovation is Simulation," *Forbes,* last modified July 15, 2013,

Obama's success was due in part to the impressive analysis accomplished by his team's simulations.

In addition to applications in leisure, education, and politics, computer-assisted simulation is a crucial element of engineering projects such as Finite Element Analysis (FEA).

Finite Element Analysis (FEA) is a method of analysis by which large, complicated systems can be understood through breaking them down into smaller components. Those small components are analyzed, and then a computer adds up the individual components into a system of equations to examine the original system. It is widely used to examine subjects such as heat transfer, structural mechanics, and fluid flow.[13]

Such an endeavor is technically complex. Simulations can be used not only to crunch the necessary numbers, but also to create animations that convey the results quickly and understandably. They can visualize weak points and potential flaws in a manufacturing product, for example, before that product is created.

Beyond political demographic analysis and FEA, computer-assisted simulation can also help businesses and organizations streamline their processes in order to increase efficiency, decrease congestion, and identify problem areas.

Consider the example of an **emergency room** (ER) with long wait times; therefore low patient satisfaction. The decision is

https://www.forbes.com/sites/gregsatell/2013/07/15/why-the-future-of-innovation-is-simulation/#58c830d515e9.

[13] Lawrence Marks and Richard Cave-Penney, Strategic Simulation and Analysis, *Introduction to Basics FEA,* YouTube video, 8:37, last modified Feb. 9, 2015, https://www.youtube.com/watch?v=_xxO_7yrg10.

made to staff more physicians and nurses there in order to alleviate this congestion. However, the problem does not go away.

A computer-assisted process simulation might examine the whole picture more closely and reveal the true cause of the delay. The simulation model shows that the physician and nurse response time are not the cause of the long delay. In fact, patient treatment and diagnosis are very efficient and are performed expediently within the ER. The simulation also reveals that the delay is caused by hospital bed shortages due to lack of bed management, and a lack of proper discharge cycle procedure.

As a result, patients who have already been treated are waiting in the ER for a bed to open up in the appropriate wing of the hospital in order to be admitted.

Alternatively, a simulation could shed light on inefficiencies in a **warehouse distribution center**. Distribution centers are complex places in which humans interact with automated machinery in many different ways. Tracking, transporting, and managing inventory can be difficult when a location handles products of varied weights and sizes. Making a change in one part of the chain can have a major effect on the output of another area. By analyzing inbound and outbound shipment requirements and schedules, simulation can provide insight on the number of workers needed, the replenishment cycle, slotting, and more.

Simulations of the warehouse's process would allow managers to test different layouts—wider aisles, different material handling equipment, and so on—without engaging in a complicated and costly trial and error period. Running different scenarios with the use of a computer program would allow the operations manager to understand how employees and machinery interact. The operations manager would be able to find the most efficient arrangement, thereby reducing waste and increasing profits.

Because computers are capable of so many different things, computer-assisted simulations can take many forms: dynamic, steady-state, 2D, 3D, virtual reality, and many more! An in-depth consideration of many of these forms follows in later chapters. Each one works best in certain contexts depending on the goals and circumstances of the people or organization running the simulation.

<u>WHAT MAKES A GOOD SIMULATION?</u>

There are many factors that determine whether a simulation is useful. Later chapters describe some of these considerations. Generally speaking, there are a few key points to keep in mind.

Any good simulation must include a baseline data set. This data is important in order to understand whether a given change helps or hurts a system's efficiency. This is true of both human-driven and computer-assisted simulations. The data must be more extensive for a computer-driven set due to the complexity of the calculations. A baseline data set is simply a full collection of information about how the system runs before any changes are made. Its purpose is to provide a point of comparison for any changes that take place later.

Much like a control group in a science experiment, the unaltered baseline data demonstrates how the original system functioned. That way, once changes are made, the manager can have an accurate understanding of their effects on any and all parts of the system.

Without a baseline, it is difficult to determine the cause of a change. Consider, for example, that one day patient discharge rates at a hospital seem faster than normal. With a baseline, the manager could see normal rates and pinpoint the cause of change. Perhaps more people than usual arrived that day with easily treatable conditions. Or, a new MRI machine has cut down on wait times.

In that same hospital, a manager without access to baseline data would be unable to see how many people normally used the MRI machine. Or the number of people who showed up with easily treatable conditions. That manager would not be able to identify what caused the increased discharge rate. Therefore, he/she would not be able to replicate it on another day.

Not only does the baseline narrow down the cause of changes, it also helps to identify if a problem is being shifted to another area; rather than resolved completely. Having a record of the "normal" state [of all parts of the system], makes it is easier to catch negative effects; that may appear unintentionally in unexpected areas.

Baseline data requirements vary by system. Both older and newer systems may need different amounts of baseline data to run effectively. This depends on the simulation software, the complexity of the system and other factors. Regardless of what kind of system is used, baseline data is a critical component of a healthy understanding of any system changes.

Simulation exercises can be fun experiments that enable individuals to think outside the box. Especially in computer-assisted simulation where graphics and animation makes the task more "game-like". The many options and outcomes are also a reason why simulation projects can fail to produce the desired outcome. It can be very time-consuming and costly—sometimes even prohibitively so—to produce a perfect or near-perfect model. Therefore, it is important to consider the acceptable range and type of errors that may occur.

Some simulation software has advanced model animation capabilities. Its displays are visually stunning and it can seem like an attractive option for a potential buyer. As pleasing as these displays may be, they are useless without the backbone of analytical power and model validity that makes a simulation worth the investment.

The best simulation is not necessarily the flashiest or the most visually appealing. Rather, it is the one that can use historical and present data to make consistently accurate predictions about future results. It is the one that does not cease to function if it encounters an outlier. Instead it can adapt to the new information and incorporate it into future tests and plans. In short, the best simulation fits its original definition quite nicely. It is the best possible imitation of reality.

Chapter 2: Process Simulations

WHAT IS A PROCESS?

Processes are the building blocks of any successful organization. ARIS Community, an online business process management community, defines a business process as "a set of related tasks or activities performed to produce a product or service."[14] To put it more simply, a process is the path of an entity from a starting point to an ending point. This definition is quite broad and can encompass the processes of many different kinds of industries.

In a **hospital setting**, a process may be an operation, starting with prepping the patient and ending with cleaning the operating room after the patient has been moved to post-op. In a **manufacturing setting**, a process may begin with the creation of a product from raw materials and end with the product being shipped elsewhere. Business processes vary as much as businesses do. In a warehousing setting, a process may begin at receiving as pallets of products are unloaded from a truck and end when with the products shipped as a customer order.

Sometimes it can be helpful to break a process down into its component parts in order to examine it more closely. To use the manufacturing example above, the process may begin with melting metal and molding it into certain shapes. Then progress to cooling it and connecting the shapes together to create a product. The product is sent through various quality checks, and then shipped to its destination. Each of those steps can be

---

[14] "Business process," *ARIS Community,* accessed June 21, 2017, http://www.ariscommunity.com/business-process.

considered a process in itself. Joined together they become a business process as a whole.

The connection of these smaller processes to create one larger process is called a "process flow." Sometimes a process flow can be smooth and efficient. An entity moves quickly and easily from one sub-process to another; without delays or damage. This is the ideal in business processes because it is profitable to have these entities transition as effectively as possible from start to finish.

Other times, a process flow can be choppy and inefficient. An entity may move from Station A to Station B, but Station B is backed up and the entity must wait to continue through the process. This wait time can range from a few minutes to a few hours depending on the circumstances. Regardless, lengthy wait times mean that the process cannot meet demand efficiently.

It is clear, then, that process flow is critical to the success of any organization. Making constant small changes in a lengthy trial and error period may lead to more harm than good, disrupting workers' routines and frustrating upper management. At this point, one would ask "How does an organization optimize its process flow?".

PROCESS SIMULATIONS

Process simulations are the solution to those concerns. By creating a computerized model of the process or processes an entity follows, a team can test out different scenarios and determine the best course of action *before* implementing it.

BENEFITS OF PROCESS SIMULATIONS

Process simulations are useful, first and foremost, for the reasons that most simulations are useful: they provide insight into how systems and processes work without the risks that real-life experimentation can have. In addition to these general benefits, process simulations also have several advantages in a business context.

One of these advantages is an excellent Return On Investment (ROI). ROI compares how much money was invested in a business or process and how much money was earned based on that investment. ROI is highest—and therefore indicates the most profit—when a small amount of money was invested and a large amount of money was earned.

Simulations allow all kinds of hypotheticals to be run and analyzed without making changes to the real-life organization. They are incredibly cost-effective. An organization only needs to invest in the software and training for their team of employees to use it. After that, simulations cut costs and find ways to make the business more efficient and profitable. For these reasons, a company's ROI for simulations tends to be quite high.

ROI is not always measured in terms of monetary profit. In some cases, such as healthcare, ROI can be measured in other ways— patient health outcomes, for example, or patient satisfaction.

Simulations still help with this non-financial ROI. Patient health outcomes, satisfaction, and many other elements can be tracked and analyzed over time. Different factors, such as wait time, discharge cycles, and length of stay, can influence these elements. Simulations can track how those elements influence change. While a non-financial ROI is harder to calculate, simulations can still provide just as many benefits in that context as they do in a financial one.

Process simulations are useful from a risk management perspective; as well. The practice of risk management is crucial for businesses. It consists of analyzing all possible options in order to minimize risk and maximize reward. Risk is inherent in every choice, of course. However, risk management seeks to bring risks to an acceptable level.

Simulation is an excellent part of a robust risk-management strategy. By its very nature, simulation is an incredibly low-risk method of finding information, making changes, and predicting results. Simulation allows for experimentation but shields the organization from the negative consequences that experimentation sometimes brings. It analyzes the present and predicts the future in order to give a more complete picture of operations. In many ways, simulation is a risk manager's dream come true.

LEAN CONCEPTS

The concept of **lean management** emphasizes the elimination of waste wherever it is present. This school of thought prioritizes value to the customer. It claims that any step in a company's process that does not add value to the product from a customer's perspective should be eliminated; if possible.

Lean concepts represent a radically different way of thinking compared to traditional processes. Rather than training employees to avoid errors in an existing process, a lean strategy would change the process so that errors are hard or impossible to commit at all.[15]

Lean thinking means manufacturing products only as customers demand them rather than producing a large supply upfront based on a sales forecast and hoping that the forecast is accurate.[16] The priority is the customer. Value is based on the customer's perspective and customer demand drives production.

Lean thinkers have coined a number of terms to describe elements of a lean process. *Kaizen* refers to slow, steady progress and continual change to create constant improvement. *Kanban* refers to an automatic replenishment strategy in order to keep inventory at desired levels. *Overall equipment effectiveness* (OEE) measures availability, quality, and performance of any machinery involved in a process in order to determine how to make those machines work as effectively as possible. These ideas are just the tip of the iceberg when it comes to the divergent thinking of a lean management strategy.[17]

Lean concepts and lean thinking are not tied to a specific industry. It is true that they emerged from manufacturing practices, but the concepts, methods and strategies that developed apply to every industry—logistics, warehousing, document flow, healthcare, and so on.

---

[15] Ibid.

[16] "Lean Manufacturing," *LeanConsultingWorks, LLC,* accessed June 21, 2017, http://www.leanconsultingworks.com/lean-manufacturing.htm.

[17] "25 Essential Lean Tools," *LeanProduction,* accessed June 21, 2017, http://www.leanproduction.com/top-25-lean-tools.html#25-essential-lean-tools.

Lean strategies have been proven to reduce operational costs and maximize the efficiency of the operation when properly implemented.

One must first understand the concepts and strategies. Then implement any relevant, beneficial strategies to the real-life environment. For example, a single piece flow does not apply in an emergency department, but it is highly efficient in car manufacturing.

Process simulations can be a great addition to lean process implementation. The lean school of thought prioritizes the elimination of waste. By going through the entire process in detail and creating a computerized model, the team gains a better understanding of any waste in the process and how to decrease it.

The actual simulation is even more useful in cutting down waste. Modelers can change different variables and run what-if scenarios as frequently as they want. Testing the effectiveness of each step of the process and examining different options to improve it. A well-built simulation allows the team to leave no stone unturned as members investigate and optimize every part of the process.

VALUE STREAM MAPPING (VSM), VALUE ADDED TIME (VAT), AND PROCESS MAPPING

Many lean concepts have been implemented with great success in a wide variety of industries. One concept in particular can be very helpful in the simulation process: **value stream mapping (VSM)**.

A VSM is a visual outline of a value stream. A value stream consists of every step that an entity goes through during a process or set of processes.[18] It may be done physically with pencil and paper or other items that can be rearranged easily, or with the aid of computer software that makes it easier to share, modify, and track changes.

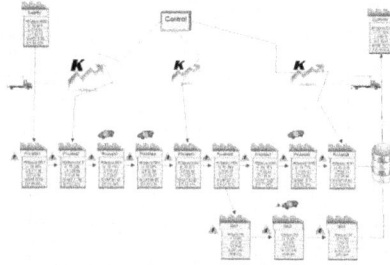

Image 1 – Sample Value Stream Map

The VSM should be constructed primarily by the team that knows the business best and is implementing the changes. By creating the map themselves, the team members gain a thorough understanding of all the steps in their organization's process. An external expert may be present alongside the team to help guide the process and assist the team members in the VSM expansion.

The key consideration in a VSM is **Value Added Time** (VAT). VAT refers to the amount of time in a process that is dedicated to adding value to the entity from a customer's perspective. Non-VAT is time dedicated to work that does not make the entity any more valuable from a customer's perspective. Non-VAT should be eliminated if possible, or at least cut down as much as workers can manage.

---

[18] Deborah Nightingale, "Fundamentals of Lean," *Massachusetts Institute of Technology,* lecture slides, September 12, 2005, https://ocw.mit.edu/courses/aeronautics-and-astronautics/16-852j-integrating-the-lean-enterprise-fall-2005/lecture-notes/2_lean_fundament.pdf.

Sometimes, non-VAT cannot be eliminated. Certain limits driven by the system layout or unchangeable process interactions may be constraints that do not add value but cannot be removed from the process. These steps must be accepted as necessary rather than considered waste; they cannot be removed without causing harm to the process flow and quality of service or product. Focus on waste removal should lie elsewhere, critiquing steps that *can* be changed.

The VSM, which examines all of the steps and interactions in a process, helps team members to identify VAT and non-VAT in the process as a whole. The detailed breakdown helps the team to pinpoint exactly what areas are causing problems.

After creating the VSM, the team can create a second map outlining changes to the current value stream. This helps the entity to flow smoother from point-to-point.

The actual creation of the VSM should not become a constraint in itself. The common practice of using sticky notes in shared conference areas may not always be the best way to expand the VSM. If a sticky note is misplaced by other users of the common areas, the team has to waste time rearranging the flow and needs to constantly validate to make sure no unwanted changes have been made.

A **process map** is similar to a VSM. Nonetheless, a process map contains less detail and focuses more on customer opinion than on waste elimination.[19] Process maps can be an important part of understanding the path a product takes because they tend to take

---

[19] "What is the difference between Value Stream Mapping and Process Mapping?" *SixSigmaStudyGuide.com,* accessed June 21, 2017, http://sixsigmastudyguide.com/value-stream-vs-process-map/.

a more "big-picture" approach. This can be a useful perspective to understand when explaining process alterations to upper management or other influential parties.

The exercise of creating a VSM or process map gives a team an in-depth perspective about the processes their organization performs. With this understanding, they can begin to build a successful simulation.

EFFICIENCY AND UTILIZATION

A VSM is designed to examine efficiency. Which parts of the process add value? Which parts can be eliminated? Lots of businesses and organizations fall into the trap of assuming that efficiency is the same thing as utilization. In reality they are completely different concepts.

Efficiency examines how well the process works. Is there waste? Does the process maximize VAT? Could the same tasks be accomplished less expensively? What changes can make this process faster, cheaper, and more intuitive? These are all questions that deal with efficiency.

Utilization, in contrast, refers to what proportion of the available resources are being put to use. Are all machines being used? Are all staff members busy? Is the organization using everything at its disposal to contribute to this process? These are all questions that deal with utilization.

The main problem with confusing utilization for efficiency is that maximizing utilization has no effect on efficiency. Using every single machine available does not mean the process is more efficient. Maximum utilization means that the organization is *busy*—every part is doing work. It does not mean that the work being done is useful. High utilization rates can still be full of waste.

The optimum state for an organization is to increase efficiency; at lower utilization. This may seem confusing at first. You might ask, why wouldn't the organization want to use every available resource?

By implementing lean concepts and trimming away waste, the organization determines how many machines are necessary to complete the desired processes efficiently, at a lower cost, and without overtaxing the operation. Once that is achieved, the organization can increase capacity without the need of adding new equipment, all while maintaining consistent lead time.

LEAD TIME

Lead time is an important measure to monitor. Lead time consists of the time required to work on an entity from the time it enters the flow until it is ready to be delivered. In a **healthcare setting**, the lead time is the patient length of stay (LOS); in **manufacturing**, it is the time required to produce the part from raw material to finished goods; and in **warehousing**, it is the time to pick an order sequence from the time it is released to be picked until it is ready to be loaded on a truck.

Lead time can also be measured at smaller intervals within the process flow. As discussed earlier, each process step can be expanded into multiple sub-steps with more detail. This breakdown means lead time can also be measured at each process step or between hand-off points within the flow.

In either of these cases, the lead time starts when an entity arrives at the process. Then continues until it starts its transition to the next process.

In **manufacturing**, it consists of the total time between arriving at the process and being added to the next conveyor. This includes all buffer wait times, manpower delays, change over, downtime, cycle time (VAT), and time spent waiting for a conveyor spot to open or a carrier to pick it up. In other words, the lead time is the total time the entity is occupying space at the process step.

The purpose of collecting the lead time of sub-processes is to identify potential areas of improvement. If the team looks at the total lead time and identifies a goal to reduce it, members must examine all the key lead times along the processing cycles in order to pinpoint problem areas. This step also aids in developing the optimal course of action to improve the flow.

The efficiency of the operation, or of a section of the flow, can be formally defined as a ratio between lead time and VAT. If VAT is the minimum time required for an entity to complete the process flow, then the operation is 100% efficient when the total lead time matches the total VAT for each step along the way.

When multiple types of entities are being processed, whether the entity is a part, a person, or a box, identifying each entity's efficiency helps in identifying the true cause of any delays. This can minimize unnecessary changes to the operation.

With all those points in mind, the goal should be to maximize efficiency and not utilization. When the operation is running efficiently, closer to 100%, the maximum capacity of the operation is tied to the utilization of the equipment, and when utilization increases, capacity increases. That is not the case when efficiency is low.

Many entities occupy space due to non-VAT—usually waiting for something to happen. An entity may wait in a buffer, wait for providers, wait to be processed, wait due to downtime, or wait to clear the process space and move to the next station.

Throughput of the operation has a direct correlation to lead time. When consistent lead times are achieved, throughput numbers are consistent. Due to entity variability, lead time may not always be consistent, but having the lead time under control with proper measures provides a more predictable, controlled throughput.

In **lean terminology**, TAKT time is a measure of how quickly an operation should complete actions on its entities from an overall throughput perspective in order to meet design specifications. If the TAKT time specifications are an entity completed every 15 minutes, for example, then the computed throughput of the operation when simulated should provide a rate that is less than or equal to that target. That computed throughput indicates that the TAKT required is achievable. On the other hand, if the computed throughput is consistently greater than target TAKT time, then the operation is taking too long. It does not meet the requirement and must be redesigned.

Efficiency and Work in Production (WIP)

The goal of a VSM, and the goal of lean processing more generally, is to increase efficiency. One common stage at which to do this is when products are complete, but waiting to be packaged and shipped. This phase is called "Work in Production," also known as "Work in Progress" or **WIP**, and it is full of opportunities to cut down on waste.

Items sitting around waiting in buffers or to be moved are wasting space, resources, and—most importantly—money. Large buildups of items in production are often symptoms of inefficiency in the process. Reducing WIP in any operation has a direct impact on cost of production. Instead of wasting money on items waiting or completed that cannot be sold, that cost is saved or applied to improve the operation itself. WIP is dollars eliminated from the business expenses and added to its cash flow.

For example, in a **hospital setting**, a patient may be cleared to leave at 9:00 AM. After waiting for the nurses to sign off on paperwork, obtaining personal items that may be stored elsewhere, and going through all other parts of the discharge process, it may be 3:00 PM before the patient actually leaves.

Those six hours are put to no use; they are not Value Added Time. Another patient could have been seen and even could have started the treatment cycle in that span of time. That room could have been used for someone else. During those six hours, the healthy patient sat, waiting for the process to catch up.

Efficiency, therefore, is not only a question of the process as a whole. It can be measured by entities flowing through the system as well. With every delay, these entities—like the patient, waiting hours to leave long after treatment has been completed—collect inefficiencies that build onto their time in the process. Lengthy WIP phases slow down the process and decrease profits.

Therefore, when attempting to increase efficiency, it is important to look at the process from the entity's point of view; not only from an impartial standpoint. Delays or bottlenecks in just one area could hold everything up. This slows down the entity's path through the process and contributes directly to problems in other areas.

AN ORGANIZATION'S MINDSET TOWARD SIMULATION

Process simulation often mistakenly takes place as a one-time event:

- A team builds a simulation for a certain purpose,
- Finds a solution to that particular concern, and
- Never uses the simulation again.

This one-time simulation use throws away the opportunity to use that same model to expand to different kinds of analysis and study future issues that may arise.

In fact, simulation can be a revolutionary element to add to daily activities at most organizations. Predicting how the events evolves on a given day. Analyzing the effect today's work has on tomorrow's operations. Considering changes to make on the fly are all benefits that a simulation can have in day-to-day use.

When a company invests in a simulation tool, its members need to learn how to use it continuously. Not only when a problem arises. Changes that a company makes to its process need to be added to the simulation in order to keep it accurate. That way, when a problem or question *does* arise, the simulation already matches the real-world environment and it can be used to make predictions without a lengthy update period.

The majority of the challenge of simulation-building comes from the actual creation of the model. Going through the effort of building an accurate computerized replica of a process only to use the simulation once and then let it sit collecting dust is wasteful. Instead, once the simulation is built, it can be used again and again to answer many different questions and predict a variety of possible futures.

- Process simulations are a useful tool. They help you examine how to make processes faster, cheaper, and more intuitive. They have a high ROI and are a low-risk option compared to trial and error; which can be costly and even dangerous.
- Simulations are also an important part of a lean management system. They can help a team visualize problems better. Then test out different solutions before implementing them in a real-life environment.
- VAT is prioritized in lean management and works to cut down on any waste or inefficiencies in the process. A VSM or process map can be a good way to view these inefficiencies in every step of the process.
- In order to implement lean concepts into a work environment, managers must understand the difference between efficiency and utilization; maximizing utilization does not automatically mean maximizing efficiency. As the saying goes, "Work smarter, not harder." In this case, the saying refers to the need to increase efficiency rather than utilization.
- One common site of inefficiencies is WIP—work in production. Completed entities that have not been shipped out take up space and resources that could have been used to drive production forward.

Chapter 3 provides a step-by-step walkthrough of building a successful simulation. This will help your team harness the full power of simulation.

Chapter 3: Building a Successful Simulation

There are many important steps in the model building process. Each one plays a valuable role. When performed correctly, the many components can lead to an efficient, useful, user-friendly simulation that provides meaningful insights into the process it emulates.

Conversely, failure to properly manage and implement the modeling and analysis aspects renders the simulation a time-consuming project; that serves no purpose. Simulation projects are driven by results based on their goals. Failure to deliver means the end of simulation modeling and a bad reputation for a very useful technology incorrectly implemented.

In order to create a successful simulation, a team must follow these five steps:

1. Define the goal by outlining question(s) the simulation is implemented to answer.
2. Collect relevant activity data for the simulation to use.
3. Build and validate the model one step at a time.
4. Run and validate the simulation.
5. Experiment, analyze, and present findings.

This chapter addresses each of the five steps in turn, since each one is a crucial element of the simulation building process.

STEP ONE: DEFINING THE GOAL

In the wise words of American speaker and author Earl Nightingale, "People with goals succeed because they know where they're going."[20] Without a clearly defined goal, it is impossible to know whether any endeavor is successful. Especially the creation of a simulation model; which must always be designed with a particular task in mind.

The goal itself can vary widely based on industry and organization. Some specific examples might be to find a solution for an existing problem, design a new assembly line, identify bottlenecks and flow constraints, determine a cell layout, load level a line, and many others. Alternatively, the goal could be more general, like improving overall operation performance, reducing manpower, designing a new facility, or improving patient flow.

In the case where the main goal is broad in nature, it needs to be refined and broken down into more attainable simplified goals. Each completed sub-goal gets the simulation project closer to accomplishing the original general goal. The details may differ and the path may vary, but the principle remains the same. Without a specific purpose, a simulation project does not deliver the desired results.

A common mistake in simulation projects' goal definition is the failure to involve the key stakeholders in the implementation. For example, if the goal of the model is to load level a production line, that task may require a rework of the flow. People that may be affected by the change need to be involved in the goal definition, as well as validation and experimentation later on. In the development of goals (and in all other parts of the simulation-building process), it is absolutely critical to communicate openly

---

[20] "Earl Nightingale," *BrainyQuote*, accessed June 7, 2017, https://www.brainyquote.com/quotes/quotes/e/earlnighti383343.html?src=t_goals.

and frequently with all others who is impacted by the simulation's findings.

In particular, the simulation goal must be clearly communicated to upper management. Upper management is often more in tune with the overall direction of the company, so their perspective may differ from that of the simulation-building team. This different perspective may complicate the goal-setting process somewhat. Regardless of convenience or good intentions, developing a simulation with an unapproved set of goals is useless. Worse, it has a tendency to generate friction and problems within the organization.

Once everyone involved has agreed on a goal or set of goals, the team should document the steps required to achieve the desired outcome. These steps serve as a guide during the creation of the simulation in order to keep everyone on track and remind the team of what needs to be done.

It is easy to discount the goal-setting stage or the importance of communicating with upper management. This early work sets the foundation for all future work on the simulation. Without proper planning and discussion, stakeholders may end up dissatisfied with the simulation later down the line. Especially when big changes are much more difficult to implement. By communicating early and often, everyone's expectations are the same and satisfaction is much easier to attain.

STEP TWO: COLLECTING DATA

Once all stakeholders are on the same page and have a clear understanding of simulation goals and the plan to get there, it is time to collect data. Simulations require a significant amount of data to run effectively, so it is crucial to complete this stage with care.

The team should obtain a facility diagram or computer aided design (CAD) layout of the premises during this time. This layout serves as the backbone of the simulation and is necessary to determine space availability and other constraints. The goal of the CAD layout is not only to create a spatial view of the facility, but also to communicate ideas, flows, and potential changes.

The CAD layout should include unmovable equipment, key beams, and other permanent parts of the facility, but there is no need to include movable items like furniture. Electrical diagrams are also unnecessary. The purpose of the CAD layout is to capture the spatial limits of the operation, including distance of transfer, without adding superfluous detail.

Data can also come from existing processes, whether that is an assembly line or an operating room. Cycle times, transfer times, required manpower, machine cycles, and machine capacities are some examples of types of data to consider. The most relevant types of data varies depending on the type of simulation and what goals the team has created for it.

Product flow details are another helpful source of data. A team should clearly define the path that an entity takes as it moves through the operation, whether that "entity" is a bottle, tire or a walk-in clinic client. It can also be useful to define product types by categorizing diverse products into common sets if they have relevant elements in common. Making decisions like this during the data collection phase can streamline the simulation-building process once the actual modeling begins.

In many cases, not all data points are available when the simulation starts. Additional data might be incorporated as the simulation develops. If one waits until every data point is available before starting the simulation modeling project, then the project never starts. Rather than engaging in a never-ending quest of data gathering, the team should identify the key data elements required for the simulation and focus on that first.

Once enough data is available to define the flow, the team should identify both cycle times and model entities to be simulated. That is the point at which the simulation project should begin. As the model is developed, additional data sets are gathered in to further define the model. When actual data is not yet available, sample data sets may initially be used. When actual data becomes available, it can be introduced into the simulation model for better representation.

Just like the goal-setting stage, documentation is often overlooked. This can have significant implications later on. During the data collection phase, it is best to document any exceptions to general rules. Keeping track of testing ratios and the quality assurance (QA) impact is important as well. All of this information is useful when building the simulation and conducting analysis.

Thorough documentation has the added benefit of helping to keep all team members updated about any pertinent information. This minimizes the potential for miscommunication and dissatisfaction later on. Different team members may consider different types of data to be relevant, and the act of discussing the potential choices helps to create the best possible data set for the simulation.

Teams must conduct data collection carefully. If the data set from which the simulation is built is not accurate, the results are not true to life. The data must correctly represent real-life processes in order to create a realistic simulation. For this reason, the data collection stage is an opportunity to think hard about what kind of information serves as a foundation for the simulation.

STEP THREE: BUILDING THE MODEL

The goal-setting and organized data collection of the previous two steps pay off during the model-building phase. Although this step may seem like the first part of the "real" simulation-building process, it depends heavily on the work of the previous two steps in order to be successful.

When building a model, the first task is to build a model skeleton. This is a basic version of the desired model that contains all the major flows. Any parts or objects that need to be tracked on their way through these flows should have already been defined in the data collection phase.

It is important to concentrate on the key components of the model at this time. These include stations or room locations, aisles, buffers and waiting areas, etc. The model skeleton does not have cycle times or constraints implemented, except those that are inherent from building the flow.

In building the model skeleton, the team must:

- Define the environment,
- Extract and define the roles of any processes involved, and
- Address inter-process connections.

Defining the environment involves the facility diagram or CAD layout of the premises obtained earlier. The physical constraints of the available space provide boundaries for the simulation.

Extracting and defining the roles of processes relevant to the simulation can be tricky. In the real world, environments are made of several constrained, interconnected processes. Translating that web of interactions into a simulation may pose a challenge. More than one virtual process may be necessary to simulate a real-world process. The key is to mimic the behavior of the real-world process as closely as possible.

Inter-process connections are also important considerations for a model-building team. Inefficient connections can be a cause of delays and bottlenecks. Incorporating accurate data into the model when examining these locations is paramount.

The final step of building the model skeleton is to perform a set of validation steps to make sure the basic model works correctly and entities flow properly. Beginning the validation process this early quickly resolves any initial errors; which prevents future complications. The resulting process creates a solid base to build the rest of the model.

Once the team has completed the model skeleton, members can introduce other properties to mimic the complexities of a real-life process. This includes timing properties like setup time and carrier loading or unloading, for example. The team should also assign QA ratios and routings at this point in the process.

It can be tempting to rush into the more "exciting" parts of model-building, such as 3D animations or visually appealing displays. However, these activities must wait until all of the groundwork is completed. This means working diligently on the model skeleton. Incorporating reliable and representative data. Communicating clearly and frequently with other team members.

The hard work may not be flashy, but it is the force by which the most reliable and useful simulations are made. The goals set in the first step of the process can be helpful here. If the team spent the proper time and attention on setting those goals, now is the time that the goals serve as guiding principles for model construction.

STEP FOUR: VALIDATING THE MODEL

The logical step after building a model is testing to make sure that it accurately reflects the real-life process it was designed to emulate. There are many different ways to compare the simulation to reality; certain tests work better than others depending on the type of model and its purpose.

A good place to start when it comes to validation is validating the model flow. This means running the simulation. Checking all object paths. Verifying the cycle times and process behaviors. There should be copious data available for comparison on all of these. Catching simple errors here can improve simulation quality significantly.

It is important to use proper data when validating a model. If the data set entered into the model is inaccurate or faulty, the results of a model—even a perfectly functioning model—is flawed. This is the principle of "Garbage In, Garbage Out" (GIGO). Common data flaws include putting too much emphasis (or not enough!) on outliers as well as failing to use historical data when it is available.

Validation should take place continuously as the model runs. Not only as one step at the end of the process. This is because if the validation tests uncover a flaw in a complex, nearly complete model, it can be difficult to pinpoint the source of the flaw. If validation tests occur throughout model development, it is easier to identify which change caused the inaccurate test results. It is also easier to fix the problem.

Once the team validates the model flow, identifies errors, and corrects them, it is best practice to verify the final model. This consists of comparing the model's results to existing data if it is available. It also involves verifying model flows, delays, and bottlenecks to ensure that reality and simulation match as closely as possible.

The model must contain all the same problems as the real-life environment because the purpose of a simulation is to test out changes to fix those problems. Validation, therefore, is not a test of how efficient the model is. It's about how closely the model emulates reality.

Communication with other team members during the validation process is critical; just like every other step. This can be a time of many changes for the model as tests reveal weaknesses and flaws to address. Maintaining open communication during this time can be difficult. However, it can help build credibility for the model which grows more and more true to life through every part of the process.

STEP FIVE: ANALYZING THE MODEL

Once the model is fully created and validated, it is time to use it for its intended purpose! One way to use the model for analysis is to run "what if" scenarios. Testing small changes one at a time helps the team understand how different parts of the simulation—and of the real-life operation—interact with each other. Plus where improvements can be made.

Testing those changes one at a time is the best way to determine their effect. Let's say the team makes two changes at once and the result is a significant improvement to overall efficiency. How can anyone tell which change it was? Or, did both changes create the improvement?

It is also a good idea to make full use of any available reporting tools in the simulation software. This varies by type. Using both process summary and simulation summary reports can provide helpful analytics; that may indicate areas of potential improvement.

As usual, the team should document any changes that they make in order to have a thorough record. If a mistake happens, it is easier to find its origin; if all changes have been carefully documented.

If the team has kept in open communication with all stakeholders, the analysis phase progresses smoothly. That means everyone understands the model's capabilities and appreciates the rigor of the testing it has undergone. Team members and C-levels are likelier to be receptive to any suggested workplace changes based on the model's findings. With team members and management involved every step of the way, C-levels understand the value of their suggestions.

If there has been inadequate or inconsistent communication up until this point, stakeholders or C-Levels may not trust the results of the model. They may be unwilling to implement suggested changes to the organization's process. If C-Levels are going to ignore the model's findings, there is little reason to go through all the trouble of creating it!

When running analyses, new issues or problems may be discovered within the simulation. It can be disheartening to find problems so late in the process. However, it is important to stay the course and to continue to work toward the goals set at the beginning.

Once a solution is found to any issue, the team should run the solution with different product mixes and resource allocations to test how effective that solution is.

As a rule, once the simulation is complete, the team should run the worst-case scenario, the best-case scenario, and the average scenario when making decisions about the future. It is a common misconception that there is no need to run the best-case scenario. In fact, if an organization is unprepared for the best-case scenario, it can run into problems when conditions are better than expected. That means the organization won't keep up. The worst-case, best-case, and average scenarios together provide the most comprehensive preparation for all the varied realities of the workplace.

In summary, there are **five critical steps** to creating a successful simulation.

1. Team members must create a set of goals for the simulation and a plan to achieve them.
2. Gather data from all necessary sources.
3. Build the model itself, starting with a model skeleton and gradually adding components to emulate real-world processes.
4. Validate the model through rigorous, continuous testing.
5. Remain vigilant as they begin to use the model for analysis purposes and make any necessary changes to bring them closer to their original goals.

Throughout the entire process, it is crucial for the team to remain in contact with each other and with all stakeholders so that miscommunications and misconceptions can be corrected; and hopefully avoided entirely.

Rigorous documentation is another necessary component of successful simulation building. Without a thorough record of changes, it is more difficult to determine the origin of errors in the simulation and misunderstandings are likelier to arise.

If all five steps are performed properly, with clear communication and documentation throughout the entire process, the resulting simulation can be a powerful tool to aid in any organization's process management.

Chapter 4: Goal-setting

Goal-setting is an exciting challenge for a team as its members embark on a simulation-building project.

During the goal-setting process, the problem at hand needs to be explained and identified as a pain point to everyone involved. The stakeholders may have differing opinions about what the simulation's purpose should be, so communication is key. The beginning of the process is a time when everyone's voice should be heard in order to identify what problems the team hopes to solve and what a solution might look like.

The team must reach a consensus on its goals and priorities early on in the process. If team members begin the project with different impressions of what the simulation is meant to accomplish, discord and dissatisfaction result. The best way to end up with a satisfied team is to reach a consensus at the beginning and keep everyone informed along the way.

As an example, the goal of the simulation model is to perform capacity planning based on equipment or space constraints. The model, data, and analysis required differs than if the goal was to determine manpower requirements. However, a capacity model can transition to a manpower planning tool as long as that change is identified as a separate milestone; within the implementation process.

Such a transition is possible; only if the team agrees on it and plans for it to happen. Putting in the work to organize a plan early on permits this kind of flexibility and prevents problems down the line.

In addition to aiding in team satisfaction, goal-setting has a significant impact on every subsequent stage of the simulation-building process.

Data collection is directly dependent on the goal of the simulation. Without a clear objective for what the simulation should accomplish, the collected data may not be relevant. There also may not be enough data collected to achieve all of the team's goals.

Alternatively, the data collection phase may take too long as the team tries to gather information that ultimately is unnecessary. Well-communicated goals and objectives streamline the data collection process and clarify the type of data required for each model development phase.

Goal-setting also shapes the actual **construction of the model**. Modelers should build and validate a model that accomplishes the tasks for which it is designed. Expanding the model to encompass unnecessary areas or details leads to longer model development times, more extensive validation efforts, and increases the data requirements for analysis. In short, costly and time-consuming work for little to no reward.

Model validation also relies on goal-setting. To validate a model, one must have a good definition of what would constitute successful completion. A specific outline of goals and expectations can be important in order to avoid being taken in by flashy, insubstantial displays that do not achieve the team's objectives.

Another important role of goal-setting is in the **presentation phase**. Presenting model results and findings to others opens up new discussions, quests for answers, and problems to solve.

Often, the simulation model starts to deviate from the original goal in order to satisfy C-Levels within the organization, rendering the simulation goal a moving target and putting the project in jeopardy. Remaining focused on the most important objectives for the simulation prevents the team from going astray in pursuit of indirect ideas during this time.

Realistically, the model may undergo multiple iterations in order to support multiple goals. Some of which might not be clear at the start. Still, one must keep in mind the original goal and avoid distractions. This focus saves time and increases the likelihood that the main priorities are achieved.

SUB-GOALS

The original goal of a simulation may be quite broad. In cases like this, it is much more effective to break the original goal down into clearly defined, manageable sub-goals in order to make sure that the original goal is fully met.

For example, the manager of a **manufacturing plant** may want to build a simulation model to study the efficiency improvement relationship among stations and optimize scheduling and manpower. Those goals are quite broad, so the implementation of the modeling and simulation environment must be split into sub-goals with more specific intentions.

If the modeling team fails to identify smaller, more attainable milestones and instead opts for a single deliverable that performs all the functionality, the modeling project becomes too general. The lack of clear checkpoints slows the process. Most likely, it is not completed in time to support the required analysis.

The fact is, the live environment always changes. Improvements are made, schedules modified, stations updated, and so on. When the model-building process extends into many months of development in pursuit of perfection in every component, the validation process never ends. These constant alterations mean that the modeling project continuously play catch-up to the real-world environment without ever materializing into a fully functional and useful simulation.

Alternatively, the same project could be controlled by breaking down the model into multiple well-defined milestones. With the modeling team in agreement regarding the internal model naming convention, the modeling aspect can be split into multiple sections. Each station or cell can be modified, tested, and validated independently.

The overall model flow throughout the plant can utilize "black boxes" representing each station with proper constraints that can be later replaced with expanded definitions built by other members. Each milestone has a goal, is validated, and can operate as an independent entity when needed. This goal-splitting approach helps achieve highly accurate results and allows for optimization within a few weeks.

CAPACITY ANALYSIS

In order to set a realistic goal, it is important to understand one's starting point. One way to gain this understanding is through performing a capacity analysis. According to BusinessDictionary.com, a capacity analysis is the "evaluation of a factory, production process or line, or machine, to determine its maximum output rate."[21]

This evaluation looks at an organization's facilities and considers the maximum possible output rate. That is, the maximum possible number of elements exiting the system during a given period. These elements can be treated patients leaving a hospital, parts produced in a manufacturing facility, or picked orders in a warehouse.

Input, in contrast, is the number of elements that enter a system. Throughput is the number of completed, successful elements that go through a system, while output includes anything that exits a system, including scrap and faulty elements.[22]

A capacity analysis can examine input, throughput, output, or any combination thereof, depending on the needs of the organization. For example, managers in a recycling company may measure input (examining the quantity of recyclables they can collect in a day) while those in a factory may measure throughput or output (to see how many parts they can produce).[23]

A capacity analysis can take the form of a gap analysis, in which the ideal is identified and steps to bridge the gap between present circumstances and the ideal standard are taken. Alternatively, it can take the form of an incremental analysis, in which the present

[21] "Capacity analysis," *BusinessDictionary.com,* accessed June 15, 2017, http://www.businessdictionary.com/definition/capacity-analysis.html.

[22] "6 Effective Ways to Improve Manufacturing Throughput," *Marlin Steel,* last modified September 28, 2016, https://www.marlinwire.com/blog/improve-manufacturing-throughput.

[23] Martin Murray, "Measuring Capacity in Manufacturing," *TheBalance.com,* last modified November 18, 2016, https://www.thebalance.com/measuring-capacity-in-manufacturing-2221213.

capacity is identified and small steps are taken to improve that present capacity in measurable ways.[24]

Once the capacity analysis is complete and the organization understands its own capabilities, there are **three major strategies** it can undertake to address demand.

1. A *lead capacity* strategy involves boosting capacity before demand strikes. That way, the organization is ready as soon as demand arrives, potentially faster than its competitors, and is not overwhelmed if orders spike suddenly. The danger of a lead capacity strategy is that demand may not rise quickly enough to compensate for the additional costs of increasing capacity.[25]

2. A *lag capacity* strategy is the opposite: it involves waiting until demand strikes before increasing capacity. This strategy is safer than a lead capacity strategy, but it may have negative consequences if demand rises suddenly and the organization is unable to increase capacity quickly enough.[26]

3. A *match capacity* strategy, in which the company tries to keep its capacity in line with demand throughout any variations, may sound like the perfect solution. It can work for some organizations, particularly with those good planning capabilities, but it only works if it predicts

---

[24] "How to assess existing capacity and define capacity needs," *LenCD: Learning Network on Capacity Development*, accessed June 15, 2017, http://www.lencd.org/learning/how-assess-existing-capacity-define-capacity-needs.

[25] Martin Murray, "Measuring Capacity in Manufacturing," *TheBalance.com*, last modified November 18, 2016, https://www.thebalance.com/measuring-capacity-in-manufacturing-2221213.

[26] Ibid.

demand properly. If not, it can have the negative attributes of both lead and lag capacity strategies.[27]

Some lean concepts have been defined and successfully implemented in order to support a balance among the three strategies and minimize the impact of variable demand on the operation.

In a factory, for example, the ultimate goal is to provide a steady manufacturing process that is, as much as possible, uninterrupted by external factors. Two main components come into play in pursuit of this goal: scheduling and supermarket implementation. ("Supermarket," or finished goods inventory, refers to a quantity of goods that can be used as a shield against unexpected changes in demand.) As an example, we'll concentrate on the **supermarket implementation** in order to determine maximum throughput.

In an environment where demand is highly variable, production schedules can be challenging to create and maintain. By understanding the internal production of the plant at the steady state, managers can determine the proper amount of finished goods inventory (supermarket) necessary to absorb the demand fluctuation.

The following images help to explain this concept more clearly. Images 4-1A, 4-1B, and 4-1C demonstrate a **"push model"** that implements a lag capacity strategy. The company determines production directly based on demand. These figures indicate that with the limited capacity of the production environment, planning production based on demand creates a huge production deficit.

---

[27] Ibid.

The organization may want to increase capacity in order to meet demand more effectively, but managers are unable to predict how much capacity to add. Unless a sizeable investment is used to expand production capacity in order for it to support the variability, production may not catch up to demand.

On the other hand, Images 4-2A, 4-2B, and 4-2C show the lean concept of a "supermarket," where production schedules are driven by a "**pull model**" system from the warehouse. As inventory levels drop, production works on replenishing the supermarket. Customer demand is directly pulled out of the supermarket, and ordered items are shipped directly without involving the extensive production process. This method provides a more controlled production environment that is shielded from demand variability. The key is to design the supermarket to be large enough to support demand without storing excess inventory.

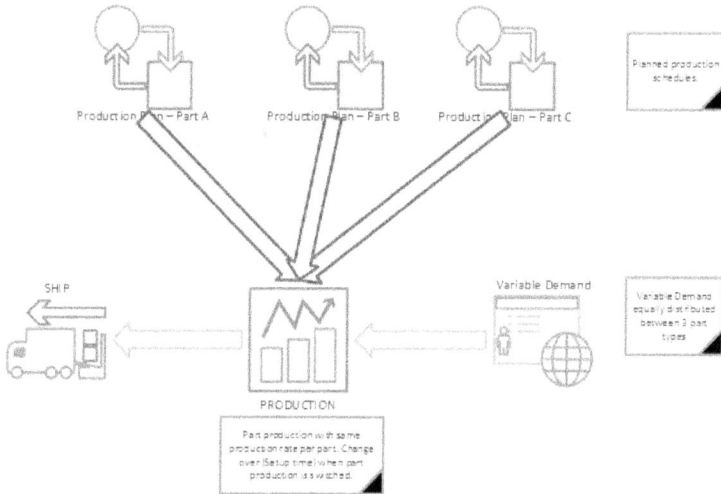

Image 4-1A. In a "push" model, limited capacity cannot keep up with variability. This type of model follows a lag capacity strategy in which production responds directly to demand.

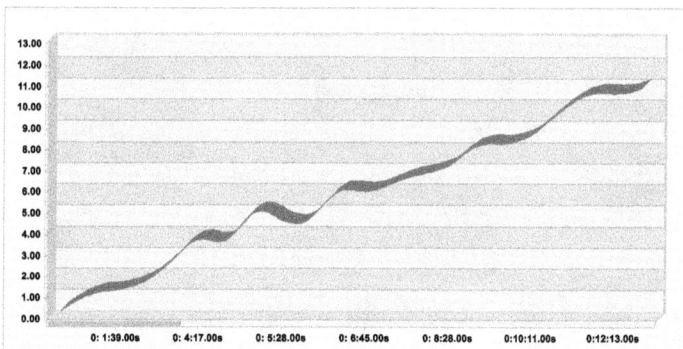

Image 4-1B. Production lead time increases constantly under a "push" model.

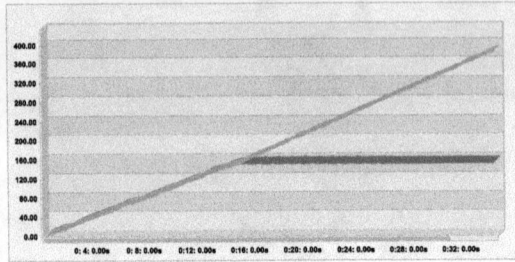

Image 4-1C. Production (blue) levels off once a "push" model reaches maximum capacity. Customer demand (green) eventually bypasses production capacity, at which point the operation is constantly running behind.

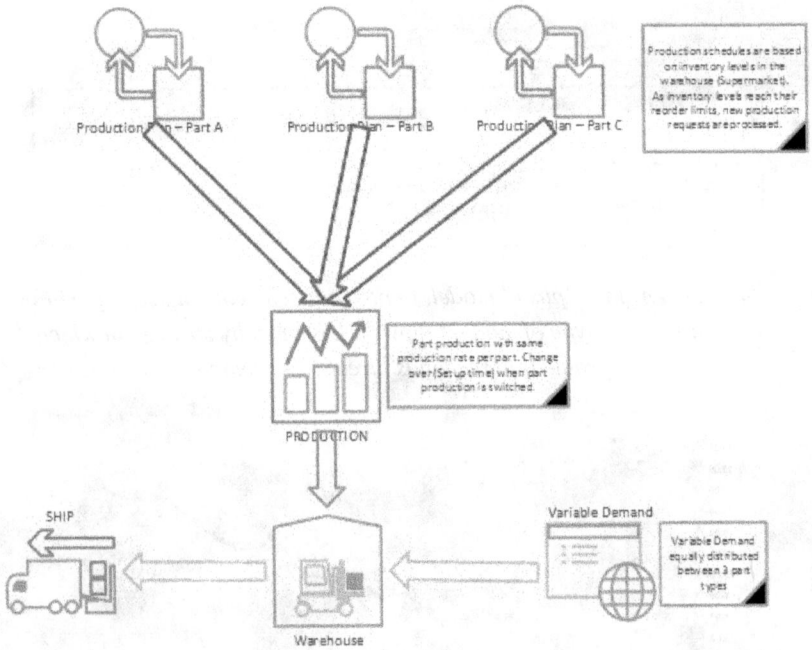

Production Plan – Part A

Production Plan – Part B

Production Plan – Part C

Production schedules are based on inventory levels in the warehouse (Supermarket). As inventory levels reach their reorder limits, new production requests are processed.

Part production with same production rate per part. Change over (Setup time) when part production is switched.

PRODUCTION

SHIP

Warehouse

Variable Demand

Variable Demand equally distributed between 3 part types

Results

By properly planning the supermarket (warehouse) size, the production environment is not affected by variable demand. Lead time for customer orders is constant and predictable. Production environment is shielded from the fluctuation. The same production capacity is used in both implementations.

Identifying the proper size of the warehouse in key in order to avoid unneeded inventory (WIP)

Image 4-2A. In a "pull" model based on lean concepts, the supermarket protects the system from variability and allows the production environment to meet demand effectively. The supermarket contains a specific, planned quantity of finished goods waiting to be shipped. When items are ordered, they are shipped from the supermarket, and the production environment responds by filling the supermarket back up.

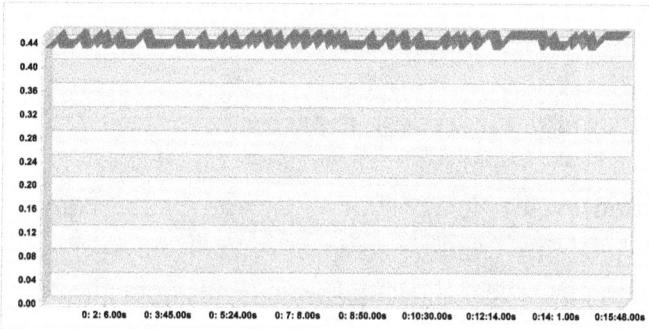

Image 4-2B. Lead time from order to shipping is constant across all three products.

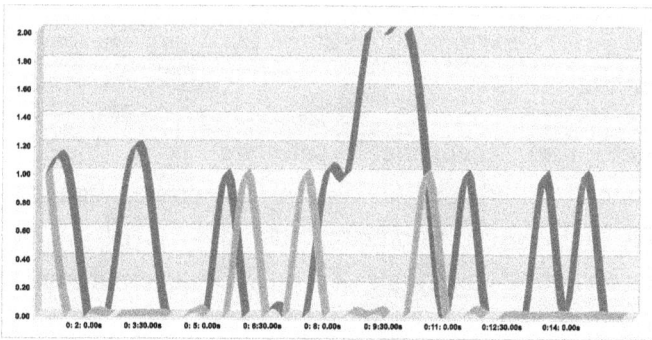

Image 4-2C. The production queue is under control. Slight fluctuation occurs, but production recovers nicely.

These figures make it clear that the same production environment is better controlled when a pull system with a supermarket is used. The capacity of the system does not change between the two models. The lead time decreases. Customer satisfaction increases. And stress levels within the plant decrease.

In a **capacity analysis model**, the environment needs to be driven to its limits using different techniques to identify maximum theoretical capacity. Attainable capacity. And minimum theoretical capacity.

The **maximum theoretical capacity** is defined as a perfect processing environment. There are no delays during the production cycle. No constraints except for the equipment or room availability. And no scrap or rework. In other words, the maximum theoretical capacity would result from all components performing at their perfect settings.

The **attainable capacity** is defined as the environment based on average constraints, including availability of equipment, processes, rooms, and a standard scrap or rework rate. Note that resource or manpower constraints <u>must not</u> be part of the constraint list.

The **minimum theoretical capacity** is defined as the environment based on maximum downtime, change over, cleaning, and rework. In other words, this consists of the worst possible operating conditions of a functioning environment.

It is critical that the modeling team and the simulation audience understand the full capabilities of the system during the goal-setting stage. This knowledge helps in identifying proper supermarket and buffer sizes in order to attain optimum efficiency.

A **sample capacity model** for eight processing stations working on three different product types may be as simple as Images 4-3A and 4-3B:

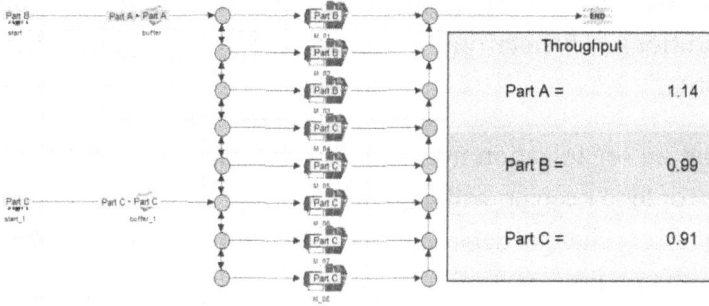

Image 4-3A. A simple capacity model with 100% OEE.

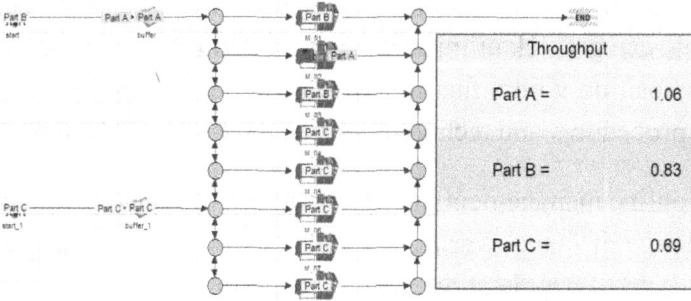

Image 4-3B. Capacity model with 80% OEE.

Even a model as basic as this can be useful in defining parameters and understanding a system's potential as well as its limits. It determines the maximum possible throughput (or output, input, etc.) in order to understand where resource constraints and other issues may be holding the process back. If team members fully comprehend the organization's capabilities and challenges, they are much likelier to develop practical, attainable goals.

MANPOWER PLANNING

Manpower is a crucial determining factor in the capabilities of many organizations. Understaffing can lead to shortages, dissatisfaction, low morale, and sometimes dangerous working conditions. Overstaffing increases labor costs and decreases profits.

What an organization needs is to have exactly the right number of people to keep up with demand safely and efficiently. Demand can often change depending on the time of day, the time of month, the time of year, and so on. It can be challenging to keep pace. Yet, if proper scheduling and capacity analysis is performed first, then variability in demand can be controlled and manpower requirements become more consistent.

In addition, people are much less predictable than machines. People can get sick or injured. They can quit their jobs or change their position within the organization. They require training for new procedures and technology as changes are implemented.

One online management instructional website aptly describes the challenge of manpower as "putting the right number of people, right kind of people at the right place, right time, doing the right things for which they are suited for the achievement of goals of the organization."[28] Planning out manpower is no small feat!

Simulations can be incredibly helpful with this process. They can prevent costly, confusing trial and error periods. They can aid in scheduling and account for projected future needs. With so many variables and considerations, computerized manpower simulations can aid significantly in keeping track of the current state of affairs as well as anticipating changes before they must be implemented.

---

[28] "Manpower Planning," *Management Study Guide,* accessed June 15, 2017, http://www.managementstudyguide.com/manpower-planning.htm.

Moreover, simulation can provide insight based on resource efficiency performing a task. When a new employee starts on a new task, there is a period of time during which the person is adjusting to the new position and their efficiency fluctuates. Studying the impact of trainees and the learning curve on efficiency is another benefit of using manpower simulation in any organization.

It is also important to take into consideration resource travel within the simulation model. Assuming that people magically transition from one station to another is unrealistic and leads to a false sense of throughput. A person needs to walk based on an identified path to and from each station or location involved in their work process. This added time constraint affects the behavior, throughput, and resource requirements of the model.

When setting goals for a simulation, it is important not to forget the influence of manpower on day to day operations. A successful simulation includes manpower and any relevant complexities or variations in how human work affects the process as a whole.

LAYOUT ANALYSIS

The spatial layout of a location is another important consideration. Processes should be organized logically in accordance with their function and the order in which events take place.

For example, a **manufacturing plant** may process a part that must move from Station A to Station B to Station C. If these stations are physically distant from each other, workers or machines need to spend time moving the piece from one location to another. This transport takes place hundreds of times every day, wasting energy and time and decreasing productivity.

Conducting a layout analysis consists of a close examination of an organization's process. Is there unnecessary distance between steps in a process? Could a rearrangement of stations, rooms, staff, or items make a process easier and more efficient? Are items placed logically and conveniently where staff can use them as needed? All of these are good questions to ask when considering making a change.

PLANNING

While setting goals, it is important not only to look at what is presently possible, but also at what changes would be needed to make improvements in the future. There are many ways to plan ahead for the needs of the future. Each of them can be helpful to consider during these early stages of simulation development.

Future capacity can be one of these considerations. If a capacity analysis determines the maximum possible output or throughput and the organization would like to accomplish more than that, then plans should be developed for how to expand the organization's capacity. This might be accomplished through construction of new rooms or facilities, for example.

Equipment planning is also important. Is the equipment satisfactory? Does it perform to the desired specifications? Does it need to be replaced soon? Are there enough machines to meet demand? Are there too many machines, and if so, can they be put to better use?

Machines can benefit from another kind of planning: **automation prove out**. Testing any automated machines under present and predicted future conditions is important in order to ensure that the machines produce the results needed. If this testing fails, the equipment may need to be altered or updated in order to make sure it is capable of accomplishing the team's goals.

COMMUNICATION

The goal-setting process is the perfect time to look at what may be slowing an organization down. That could be capacity problems. Inefficient use of manpower. Flaws in the spatial layout of a room or building, or other issues. This is the time to be critical and to identify problems; that the simulation helps to address.

The whole team, C-Levels, and all relevant stakeholders should be in clear communication during this goal-setting period. This is an important time to get everyone's input about what changes should be made. What should be kept the same? And what the simulation should do to help with these ideas?

If C-Levels are not included in this process, the whole simulation may end up being a waste. Those in authority are less likely to trust results that they did not help to design. If they are involved from the beginning, they are much likelier to drive forward the implementation of the recommendations generated by the simulation effort.

RECAP

It is important not to discount the goal-setting stage. While the team may be eager to start on the actual model-building as soon as possible, a large amount of critical work takes place during the goal-setting and data collection stages. It is this early work, often undervalued or forgotten, that sets the foundation for a successful simulation.

In addition to the simulation-related benefits that clear goal setting provides, there are benefits to the organization itself outside a simulation context. The goal-setting stage prompts the organization to begin to ask specific questions about how its operations work. Why are things done the way they are? Is it necessary to perform certain parts of the process before others? Does every activity add value, or are there some parts of the process that can be reduced or eliminated?

The team is forced to think critically about why they do what they do. If a new system is to be implemented, the goal-setting stage encourages the team to question it. How do new processes interact with old ones? Is the addition helpful? If so, in what ways?

These questions already improve the operation, even before the simulation is built.

The goal-setting stage is complete when all team members and stakeholders have agreed on the main priority or priorities of the simulation. They have discussed what success looks like, including any changes in capacity strategy, manpower, machinery, and layout. They have an understanding of the steps ahead of them, and they are ready to progress to the next stage: data collection.

Chapter 5: Data Collection

The second step in the simulation-building process is data collection. In this step, the team collects baseline information relevant to the process that is to be modeled. This background information is used to make sure that the simulation matches the real-life process as closely as possible. For that reason, data must be taken very carefully from all parts of the process.

Goal-setting forms the ideological backbone of the simulation, dictating what its purpose is and what capabilities it must have. Data collection, in contrast, forms the numerical backbone. The data collected in this stage shapes the model, outlining its constraints, probabilities, and predictions.

The importance of data collection is often succinctly described by the saying, "Garbage In, Garbage Out (GIGO)." The meaning of this phrase is that even if a model is perfectly designed, entering "garbage," or flawed input data, results in a "garbage" output that does not accurately predict real-life circumstances.

The task of the data collection team, then, is to find complete, accurate, and representative data that lead to a useful output with strong predictive power. There are many sources from which the team might choose to take this data.

HISTORICAL DATA FROM EXISTING SYSTEMS

Taking data from existing systems is a reliable, straightforward way to learn how those systems function during day-to-day operations. Enterprise resource planning (ERP), electronic medical records (EMR), warehouse management systems

(WMS), and other similar sources all contain useful historical data.

This data sometimes exists within the machinery involved in the operation. Some machines can keep a chronological record of throughput, downtime, maintenance, and other attributes over a certain period of time. Historical data, whether from machines or from external sources like hospital records, is excellent for use in simulations because it can create what are known as "apples-to-apples" comparisons between different what-if scenarios.

Comparing two what-ifs with the same set of historical data, such as that taken from records of what a machine did in a day, makes it easier to identify improvements. It is better, when possible, to "compare apples to apples". That is, to use available historical data to maintain analytic consistency. The alternative, using different data sets to compare different what-if scenarios, leads to less conclusive findings.

For example, consider a simulation designed to rearrange an emergency department's configuration to increase efficiency. The best practice would be to run historical data through the original configuration, then run the *same* historical data through the simulated redesign. By using the same set of data, including patient arrivals, acuity, treatment, and other attributes, the two configurations can be compared fairly. This "apples to apples" comparison ensures that the differences in the two sets of results are due to the configurations themselves, not data variability. After proving that the new optimization works for existing known conditions, data variability may be introduced in order to confirm the validity of the implementation.

An added benefit of using historical data from existing systems becomes clear when trying to convince stakeholders and managers to adopt the changes supported by simulation trials. The stakeholders, who may have grown accustomed to the usual way of performing the operation after many years of production, may be reluctant to make the suggested changes. By providing known data set scenarios that everyone is familiar with, the model development team can explain the benefits of change using information the group already understands. In addition, the use of historical data prevents workers from opposing the change by poking holes in the data set or distributions generated from it.

TRACKING SYSTEM DATA

If historical data is unavailable or insufficient, there are plenty of alternatives. A team might take new data by implementing a tracking system. This kind of system uses RFID, GPS, phones, Bluetooth, and other kinds of technology to track the movement of people and equipment throughout the facilities of an organization.

At face value, this kind of data may seem deceptively simple. Knowing where everyone and everything goes over the course of the day is helpful, to be sure, but how might the team figure out how often machines are used and how much downtime occurs? How can team members improve their process if they don't know how much waste time needs to be eliminated?

The answer to these questions is that tracking data can be used to determine what equipment is in use at what times. The data collection team can come to these conclusions by examining who is present with a machine at a certain time.

For example, in a **hospital setting**, there may be a machine designed to test some aspect of a patient's health. This machine can only be used by a trained technician. If the tracking data reveals that the machine, the technician, and the patient are all together for a period of time, then it follows that the machine was in use during that time.

In the case where the patient and the machine are together without any technician present to run the tests, or if the technician and the machine are together without a patient, it can be concluded that the machine is not in use. Tracking system data can therefore be used to supplement or replace historical data from existing systems due to the useful inferences that the data collection team can make.

When using a tracking system, or even when using historical data, a CAD layout of the facilities can be incredibly helpful. Not only does the CAD layout provide clear spatial boundaries for the simulation to follow, but it can also be used to identify the distance of transfer between stations.

The distance between stations is a critical aspect of the simulation and has a major impact on the overall flow. Without proper transfers between stations, there exists a huge timing gap. This gap throws off analysis by indicating that components are already present at a station when in reality, they are still in transit.

The same applies to **manpower implementation**. A worker may need to walk among multiple stations, or a nurse may need to walk from room to room in order to reach a patient. The transition time impacts the model's findings about utilization, scheduling, and throughput.

Eliminating or forgetting to include the transition behavior increases the perceived throughput, since workers are perceived as moving much more rapidly through their tasks than they really are. This renders the simulation results incorrect.

A CAD layout can therefore complement tracking data, or it can be used independently to provide important structure for the simulation in the absence of tracking data.

VENDOR SPECIFICATIONS

This section relates to **new equipment** that needs to be added or a **new system design** where actual machine performance is not yet known within the constraints of the system. In this case, historical data and performance metrics are not available. In addition, there is no concrete data set that identifies how different pieces of equipment interact. The impact of that interaction on the efficiency of the system is unknown.

In cases like this, a data collection team might choose to rely on claims from the vendor as to how the equipment performs. This data can be sufficient for a functioning simulation. Though rarely as accurate as historical data. As long as the data collection team uses common sense and performs due diligence during the analysis cycle they can determine the true limits of the systems.

Vendors often oversell the capabilities of their machinery. This is not surprising: it is a vendor's job to convince people to buy those products. The vendor usually claims that the machinery runs at 99% capacity consistently, when in truth no product ever performs at that level under real-life constraints.

In fact, the vendor is stating the performance of the equipment in ideal conditions: the environment in which the equipment was tested. The vendor specifications are actually providing the maximum attainable throughput of the system.

Therefore, if team members plan to use vendor specifications as simulation data, they must attempt to ascertain the influence of human factors and machine interactions on the stated efficiency level. Simply using the specifications without investigating what might influence them, leads to inaccurate model results. The team should engage critically with this information. Then come to common-sense conclusions before accepting vendor specifications as data.

TIME AND MOTION STUDIES

In a situation in which historical data, tracking, and performance metrics are all unavailable, **time and motion studies** are required in order to collect timing data on the process flow. It may be helpful to perform time and motion studies as a team. Have each member measure different metrics and processes throughout the operation.

For group time and motion studies, it is important for the team to agree on the data points being collected for each process step. The collection needs to capture the entity type (patient, part, pick, etc.) and the factors that interact with it. Unfortunately, most time studies look only at the process itself and fail to note the external conditions on the process. These can provide valuable insights into any delays that might take place.

Time studies are most helpful for a simulation if the process is broken down into its components instead of measured simply from start to finish. For example, in an operating room, the patient is prepped for surgery. Doctors perform the surgery. The patient goes into post-op. Then the OR is cleaned. Measuring each of these steps separately is better than measuring the time only from prep to cleaning; since separately it is easier to identify inefficiencies in the process.

The conditions of a time study must be rigorously controlled. There should be nothing new or unusual in the environment. The workers should be accustomed to their jobs and working at their normal pace. And, all machines should be working at their usual capabilities. This standardization helps to create a baseline that the simulation can use to predict the effects of potential changes.

The actual practice of collecting time data can take place with many different types of technology, from stopwatches to video cameras.[29] The sophistication of the technology one uses depends on the particular circumstances of the process being timed.

It is important to have a large sample size of data. That is, to time the same processes many times in order to determine consistency and averages. With too small a sample size, it can be difficult to identify outliers, and the margin of error can be large. If one's margin of error is too high for one's needs, it is best to increase the sample size in order to decrease the margin of error.[30]

Time studies are relatively simple to collect for machines, but in the case of human workers, there is an important extra consideration: if the data is to be accurate, the workers must not know they are being watched. It is human nature to perform differently under scrutiny, but these differences can create inaccuracies in the simulation. For this reason, time data must be

---

[29] Nikhila C, "Time Study: Definition, Procedure and Methods," *Business Management Ideas,* accessed June 13, 2017, http://www.businessmanagementideas.com/production-management/work-measurement/time-study-definition-procedure-and-methods/7162.

[30] Larry Holpp, "Preparing to Measure Process Work with a Time Study," *iSixSigma*, accessed June 13, 2017, https://www.isixsigma.com/methodology/business-process-management-bpm/preparing-measure-process-work-time-study/.

collected without the knowledge of the workforce in order to avoid interfering with the usual flow.

CYCLE TIMES

The "**cycle time**" of an entity at a processing station is a critical piece of data to measure. It is the time required to run the process, as determined by key metrics. It is not the same thing as perceived time to complete the task.

The cycle time should *only* include VAT. This is the amount of time required to add value to the entity so that it is ready to move to the next station. In other words, if there are no external constraints on the process, the cycle time is just the time required to run the process. Provided, every step of the way, the entity grows in value.

In general, when an entity arrives at a station, it goes through a simple three-step cycle:

- waiting to be processed,
- being processed, and
- waiting to proceed to the next station.

Only the second step, "being processed," counts toward the cycle time.

Waiting to be processed may involve waiting for resources to arrive, availability of the station, a required pre-setup or change over, etc. But these are *constraints* on the processing of the entity; they are not directly related to the true cycle time of the process itself! Wait time is therefore not included in cycle time.

LEAD TIME

Lead time refers to the full amount of time it takes from when an entity begins a process until it leaves the process. Lead time includes both VAT and non-VAT. In lean metrics terms, the process efficiency is at 100% when the cycle time and the lead time of the process are equal; in that case, there is no waste in the operation.

It is important not to confuse efficiency with utilization. As described in Chapter 2, efficiency is a measure of waste, while utilization is a measure of capacity. A process could be 100% utilized but 20% efficient, meaning the process is running at full capacity, but there is a great deal of waste within its constraints and related processes. The process could increase throughput or output by utilizing the same resources in a way that produces less waste.

The rest of the time it takes for the entity to go through the process is a constraint defined by availability and behavior of the overall system. This time can vary as the system changes, so rather than entering this wait time as data, it should be left up to the simulation to determine based on the performance of the other components of the system.

The model's calculated wait time should match the data the team has collected about real wait times in the system. Wait time is therefore a measure of model *validity*, not model input. This concept is discussed in more detail later in this chapter.

ARRIVAL PATTERNS AND ENTITY START SEQUENCE

The "arrival pattern" or "entity start sequence" of a process refers to the type of entities and frequency of their arrival at the start of the process flow to be treated, manufactured, distributed, or otherwise taken care of.

In a **warehouse implementation**, the arrival pattern may refer to shipping and receiving trailers to load and unload goods. Arrival data include information about the type of load, product information, size, quantity, and any other aspect that may be required for the process flow.

In **manufacturing**, the entity start sequence may be the throughput of the initial process in the sequence or the performance of the first cell. The entity start sequence could also consist of customer orders that are driving production schedules. Or, it could be determined by Kanban pull requests from product consumers.

In a **surgical department setting**, the arrival pattern can be determined by looking at the planned patients' schedules. The types of surgeries performed, and the full schedule of patient arrivals. Each patient differs in acuity, condition, surgery type, and time of arrival to the operation room area.

The method or type of scheduling (e.g. block, open, or a combination of both) is not part of the arrival or start sequence. Instead, it is a scheduling or process flow constraint. The actual schedule of patient arrivals itself is a part of the arrival pattern. The collection of the patient schedules and related properties such as surgery type constitute the arrival pattern for the surgical department.

Arrival patterns are important to include in the simulation data because they provide information about how many and what kind of entities the process deals with at a given time. They can also help in computing future capacity increases by complementing capacity analysis data.

Arrival patterns are affected by seasonality, major events, weather conditions, and other external conditions. The data collection team needs to account for all of this variability and make sure enough data is present to represent the full spectrum of conditions. Events that are not part of the norm need to be documented so they can be run as scenarios during the analysis phase.

When performing the simulation validation and analysis later in the development cycle, particular segments of the data set may be used for specific runs. In an environment where seasonality impacts the input data set, for example, it is important to have the data segmented correctly so that the validation phase has the ability to validate each season and the transition between seasons.

Similarly, studying the impact of an extreme condition should include data sets that encompass pre- and post-event data in order to understand the full causes and effects of that condition. The key is that the segment used must be comprised of data points that fit the analysis scenario.

Therefore, if an emergency department is studying the steady state of a summer month, then a few months of summer data may be introduced and analyzed. On the other hand, if the analysis is looking into the variability impact on the transition from spring to summer, then at least one month of each period need to be included in order for the simulation to represent this variability accurately. In a case where pre-loading of the model is available, then less data may be introduced that represents the pre-condition scenarios.

REWORK, SCRAP, PROCESS SELECTION

Process steps are not perfect; they sometimes fail and require additional steps to remedy the errors. This applies to all industries and all process types. A set of tests may need to be rerun for a patient, a part may need to be reworked after a manufacturing process, and a pallet may need to be repositioned on a rack. All of these represent rework operations.

In some cases, the reworked entity needs to be thrown out of the process and replaced with a new one. In **healthcare**, a second blood draw may be needed. In **manufacturing**, the part is scrapped and replaced with another good part. And in **warehousing**, a pallet may need to be rewrapped due to failure of the first wrapper.

Those data points are as important to the simulation data set as the cycle times. The introduction of failures in the system prompts capacity and throughput numbers to change. Process and entity efficiencies are also reduced because all of that rework and scrap is considered non-VAT. Increasing quality in a process therefore leads to increases in efficiency.

Another aspect of rework is selecting the next-destination process constraints. There are many ways an entity can proceed to the next process: randomly identifying an open process to go to, checking for the least busy station, evenly distributing the work, filling buffers in sequence, using preset distributions, etc. Data from real-life practices is necessary in order to input these next-destination constraints.

Note that both scrap/rework and destination selection need to be easily accessible to the analysis team in order to perform what-if scenarios and identify the changes that have the most impact on the process flow. This data is important in multiple stages of the simulation-building process.

FAILURES, AVAILABILITY, MAINTENANCE

Equipment requires regular maintenance if it is to run at optimum performance. Still, even if the team perfectly performs all maintenance as recommended by the manufacturer, equipment can fail during the process run.

Each piece of equipment has a Mean Time Between Failure (MTBF) and Mean Time To Repair (MTTR). MTBF is generally defined as the number of cycles the process goes through before requiring some type of maintenance that stops its processing. Once it fails or breaks, the equipment requires MTTR to recover from the failure and return to processing.

Any entities affected by the failure may need to be scrapped or reworked, but they also may be able to continue onto the next station. The path of each entity depends on the type and extent of machine failure.

In some cases, the only available data set is the percent availability of the equipment or its OEE. By capturing the OEE or availability of the equipment, one can avoid the need to capture MTBF and MTTR. The only downside of such practice is a slight variance introduced into the data set, which reduces the accuracy of the model. It is up to the modeling team to identify when full MTBF/MTTR should be entered in place of availability percentages.

Some failures may occur at wider intervals (once every two weeks, for example). In that case the failure should be run as a scenario in order to study the recovery period and the impact on other processes. Such a failure can be correctly studied by a model only when the internal run time of the model exceeds the failure cycle by at least 4 times. Therefore, to correctly study a biweekly failure occurrence, the model run time should be at least 8 weeks.

Failure and availability information is required for final model validation. Not, for initial model development. Because of this, the modeler should not wait for this data to be available before starting the model development.

FLOW RELATED DATA

Flow related information is critical for proper model development. Flow related data transitions the model from a basic flow model to a properly functional environment that represents the real-world state. The data collection team must gather any available routing information, containment data, constraints to transition, and information on carriers or entity movers. All of these are necessary to include complete and accurate transitions in a model.

In some cases, flow-related data may be highly complex, and it may include constraint or event detail that, in reality, is not part of the flow data set. This situation occurs when interviews are conducted with people running the operation and are directly involved in the process. Events that may have affected them in recent times seem like relevant flow-related information. In reality, they are scenario events that need to be analyzed independently.

As an example, personnel may have improvised a solution to share a piece of equipment in the last two weeks due to the fact that one of the units failed and is undergoing repair. This improvised scheme may be a temporary solution created to bypass the temporary shortage units. Yet, it is described as a potential flow requirement due to the fact that it is a recent event that required special handling. It is up to the modeling team to identify the proper flow data set and to form a proper understanding of the operation.

In other cases, routing information may be highly complex, especially in a high mix operation where each entity may follow a different route. Examples of high mix operations are manufacturing job shops, component assemblies, emergency rooms, and large clinics. In these operations, entities vary widely and take many different paths. There is often a very large data set to encompass this complexity.

The flow-related data set may be too extensive to enter into the model manually. An option in this case can be to import a data set for routing lookup instead. The modelers should make a decision early on in the development cycle about how to handle the entry of flow-related data.

COMMON DATA ERRORS

Errors in data input can cause significant problems for model validity. Entering this erroneous data leads to issues down the line—garbage in, garbage out. By identifying common data input mistakes, simulation designers can correct these errors or even prevent them from occurring.

Incorrect input data can cause a model to have incorrect results even if its behavior is correct. For example, entering the incorrect cycle time for a process changes the overall results of the model, even while the items' behavior as they progress through the model remains unaffected. Choosing the correct data set and proper input parameters is key to model validation.

One common input error has to do with **buffer wait times**. Some simulation models introduce fixed buffer wait times in order to force validation of the model. While to some this practice may seem harmless, anyone who wants their simulation to represent the real world properly should avoid this course of action at all costs.

If the purpose of a model is to cut down on wait time, wait time cannot be entered as a fixed quantity. The model is meant to predict what effect certain changes have on wait time, so wait time must be a dependent variable in the process. Entering a fixed wait time means that changes to the process do not alter the wait time, which defeats the purpose of the simulation!

During the model optimization phase, changes to the process flow should impact the wait time, hopefully reducing either the time itself or its impact on the overall lead time of the items in process.

In addition to forcing buffer wait times, a second common data input error is using **standard distributions** instead of actual data variability. Standard distributions are a handy shortcut, but what is gained in convenience is lost in accuracy. A simulation's usefulness is directly dependent on how closely it can imitate reality, so the natural variations in real-world data are very important.

A third mistake is to put too much emphasis on **outlying data**. It is important to use the correct data points at the correct times. When using a full set of historical data, the team should run the data as is; the inclusion of all the data points is to provide the most accurate representation of reality.

When using a distribution, the outliers should become scenarios rather than remaining part of the main data set. The outliers should not be discarded, of course, because they represent potential conditions that may occur again. But they should be run as scenarios rather than included within a distribution for the highest level of accuracy.

RECAP

The data collection phase is critical to the development of a simulation. Data is what allows the model to predict the future and compare different what-if scenarios. The type of data a team should collect may vary, but some dependable options discussed in this chapter are historical data, CAD layouts, cycle times, time studies, arrival patterns, scrap and rework data, MTBF and MTTR data, OEE and percent availability of the equipment, and flow related data.

It is important for the team to engage with the data properly. This means using buffer wait times as a validation tool rather than forcing wait times into the simulation. It also means using real historical data rather than statistical distributions when possible, as well as using outliers as potential scenarios rather than including them in the main data set.

The data a team uses directly affects every part of the simulation. Even if a model is designed perfectly, entering faulty data leads to inaccurate, useless results. The data collection team must take its job seriously by identifying the needs of the simulation developers and the best data available to fit those needs. The developers can then use that data to begin the actual process of model development.

Chapter 6: Model Building

Beginning the model-building phase is an exciting time in the process of creating a simulation. At last, all of the goal-setting and data collection can combine to form a visible result. The fruits of the team's labor finally begin to show. It is critical not to rush to this stage, as exciting as it may be. The backbone of planning, research, and data collection is what makes this phase and the rest of the simulation-building process successful.

Before the model-building phase begins, team members should familiarize themselves with the software they are to be using to build the model. This can take place through training, mentorship, hands-on practice, or a combination of the above, but it is important that team members understand the full capabilities of the technology they are using. Simple mistakes can have stressful consequences, so learning the ins and outs of the model-building program has a major impact on simulation development.

It is also important not to assume that all software tools are the same or use the same constructs. Many modelers who are familiar with tools that require a lot of programming turn to the coding environment before investigating the tool's capabilities. Today's simulation software contains constructs and interfaces that accomplish many of the more complicated modeling tasks with ease. Modelers must take some time to learn how to use their tools properly and effectively before embarking on a model-building project.

Many recent graduates are exposed to some type of simulation tool in college. Keep in mind that tools normally used in a college setting are not driven to speed up model development. In most cases, they rely too much on coding to build the models.

Moreover, some tools still utilize old technologies. Unlike newer modeling software, these older tools are often unable to allow validation and model-building to take place while the simulation is running.

It is difficult to overstate the importance of proper tool selection. These should be driven by the goals and time frame of the modeling project. Some software tools require extensive work to validate models so that they can be used successfully in the industry. These can extend the time frame of the project beyond what is feasible.

This increased time can pose serious problems to the creation of a simulation. A warehouse model that takes a year to build, for example, is almost useless; the real-life environment may have changed by the time the model is completed. A long model development time means that the development team is constantly trying to catch up to the live environment. Or worse, performs analysis based on a state that is no longer valid.

Considerations before building the model

The first part of a process to enter into the software is the basic flow, which has already been identified either using a basic process flow diagram or VSM during the goal-setting stage. Either way, the modeling team needs to understand the process flow being modeled. In order to enter the basic flow, the team must identify at least three elements.

First, what entities are processed? The entities consist of parts, patients, carts, boxes, tubes, or any other element the environment processes. Entities may also have relationships with other entities in the process. For example, a box may contain ten parts, or a cart can transport a pallet, or a transport chair can carry a patient. Entity relationships need to be defined early on in the process in order to avoid potential modeling rework later on in the development cycle.

Second, what are the key parameters for each entity? Parameters in a healthcare setting might include attributes like patient acuity, gender, and age. In a **manufacturing setting**, it may be more important to include object weight, color, or routing data. In a **warehouse setting**, some key parameters might be object dimensions, weight, and pick sequence. These are only examples; each project has a different set of parameters. Software tools vary widely in their ability to accommodate these parameters, from having only the most basic setting of an entity name to including a detailed set of properties with statistical data tracking for each entity.

Some types of software make it difficult to add parameters later in the model-building process, so it can be important to identify the key parameters early. Any modeling team, regardless of experience, can encounter a situation in which the model has evolved and parameters must be added, altered, or deleted. (Less experienced modeling teams are particularly susceptible to this risk.) Choosing a more open software tool that allows for parameter modifications and constantly modifies its internal data to accommodate changes can make the model-building process much easier. A team's software should help, not hinder, the development of a changing simulation.

Third, what is the internal model time resolution? The time resolution impacts the accuracy of the model. It may take one minute to move a pallet from one location to another, two minutes for a patient to move from pre-op to the operating room, or a sub-second for a photo eye on an automation line to be triggered. The time units that the modeling team chooses are very important; for the first two examples, the time unit resolution can be a second, but for the third, it must drop down to a fraction of a second.

It is important to set the model time resolution to the lowest unit that needs to be tracked. This setting allows the team to capture all potential events in the simulation run. Using an incorrect time resolution can lead to errors in the final results.

Some software includes dynamic time scaling that allows users to quickly change the time resolution without having to change the process cycle times or make substantial changes to the model. Dynamic time scaling is preferable to fixed timing models, as it enables users to modify the time resolution in order to achieve optimal results.

After determining the answers to these questions, choosing a software that suits the team's needs, and taking some time to become familiar with the functions and features of that software, the team is ready to begin building the basic flow.

BUILDING THE BASIC FLOW

The goal of basic flow buildout is to create a flow that represents the current operation without imposing any constraints or cycle times. The main focus is to build a high level representation; it can be expanded with constraints later on.

In a **hospital setting**, for example, the basic flow of a new patient could be the following:

- the patient enters the waiting room,
- is moved to triage,
- goes to an ED room,
- gets admitted,

- proceeds to pre-op,
- followed by surgery,
- post-op,
- then back to a bed before being discharged.

The team has already created a VSM or a process flow diagram in the goal-setting stage to clarify the connections between these different places and the time the patient takes in each one.

In a **manufacturing setting**, the basic flow may include:

- a set of parts, each going through a set of processes,
- then through a set of assembly operations,
- a heat treat, a paint process, etc.

The key is to capture the journey of the parts through the system.

In a **warehouse setting**, the basic flow may be:

- a bit more complex and
- include the rack definition as well as
- the picking or put-away path that is to be analyzed.

Regardless of industry, in cases where automation is present, the building process is similar. When building the basic flow, modelers should not yet include flow constraints; these constraints should only be added after the basic flow is validated.

It is important to point out that all operations require some type of buffering or queue that builds up at some point as the simulation develops. Buffers are holding stations until the entity can move to the next operation.

- a waiting area in an emergency department is a buffer,
- a set of pallets waiting to be picked up is a buffer, and
- a set of parts waiting to be processed is a buffer.

Including buffers is necessary for an operation to be accurate.

In a simulation, buffers should never have a time associated with them. The reason for this rule is that time spent in buffers is not required for the completion of the entity. The simulation is designed to make the process more efficient, so creating a model that forces entities to spend time in unnecessary process steps is counterproductive.

In other words, if a drying line is required for the process, it may be *viewed* as a buffer, but it is still critical to the overall processing time. On the other hand, a set of parts waiting to be processed is not a critical part of the overall processing time—quite the opposite. Buffer time is waste time in the process flow and must be eliminated when possible.

As a reminder, models should not include forced wait times. Entering a fixed wait time into the model means that the model does not adapt its wait times based on other influential circumstances—it just assumes the input wait time in all cases. This serious error leads to flawed results. (For more on forced wait times, review Chapter 5: Data Collection.)

The team should validate the basic flow immediately after creating it. While validation is its own stage in the simulation-building process, it is very helpful to validate *during* the creation of the model. This helps catch small, easily fixed errors before those errors go on to influence other parts of the simulation. (For more on validation, see Chapter 8: Model Validation.)

EXPANDING THE BASIC FLOW

After the basic flow is validated, the team can begin to introduce some of the constraints identified using the VSM, process flow, and collected data.

It is easiest to introduce and validate constraints using dynamic, on-the-fly software. Static or traditional tools require more starting and stopping. On-the-fly software allows the team to implement changes and validate them while the model is running; thereby shortening the development cycle by up to 50%.

Using static tools to enter constraints requires many steps.

- Team members must add a constraint,
- Stop the simulation, and
- Then validate the simulation results before moving forward.

The team needs to be careful to introduce constraints and changes one at a time in order to validate every change made.

In contrast, in an on-the-fly environment, the validation and data entry occur during the simulation run, and the results of the changes are displayed in process analysis. The modifications can therefore:

- Take effect with less data-entry time.
- Team members can simply run the software and introduce constraints into the system one by one.

Members should still watch the influence of each constraint carefully to ensure that it matches the real-life process, but there is no need to stop and start the model repeatedly then wait for the constraint condition to occur.

The time savings are even more apparent when routing or transition logic is implemented and tested. In an on-the-fly simulator, the changes are immediately displayed through the animation aspect. Plus routing can be validated at the time of change. Any tweaks or modifications can also be viewed and analyzed instantaneously.

ADDING CYCLE TIME TO THE BASIC FLOW

When beginning to add constraints to the basic flow, cycle time should be incorporated first. The team should already have this data from the data collection step performed earlier. The cycle time at each process is comprised of the VAT at that process plus any additional time required for the process to run.

For example, in a **manufacturing setting**, a piece of equipment has a load time, a cycle time, and an unload time. Although loading and unloading time at the process is considered non-VAT, the time duration is required for the operation to complete its activities on the part and should be entered and accounted for separately.

The same applies to **healthcare**: a patient needs to be helped upon arrival to the room, during the treatment, and when treatment completes. Assisting the patient to the bed and the discharge cycle are the non-VAT, and the treatment time is the VAT associated with that patient. All of this required time should still be incorporated into the model.

In some operations, the cycle time is identified as a rate instead of actual time. For example, 15 boxes per minute. Some tools allow the cycle time of the process to be entered as a rate instead of a straight time; in that case, the entity time and unit of time need to be defined. Otherwise, the rate needs to be converted to time per entity; in our example, 4 seconds per box.

If the process contains some variability in the timing, the process cycle may be entered as a distribution that averages out to the actual cycle time. One 4-second cycle per box could be entered as a normal distribution with a range of 3 to 5 seconds providing an overall average of 4 seconds, but with a slight variation in the output rate. (This variation must not be confused with changeover or product variability, as those are considered separate constraints entered later on in the process.)

When more complex data timing is required, the modeler needs to fit the data set to a distribution curve that represents the variability of the set. In the case where the modeler opted for a simplified distribution in this step, the distribution must be changed to the correct representation before the analysis phase can start.

Any timing variability or curve fitting also needs to be performed as part of this step. A timing distribution does not and may not follow a known distribution set. It is imperative that the modeling team avoid forcing the data set to fit a known distribution. This is a limitation of the software being used and should not be introduced into the model. Any data distribution or curve fitting environment must find the polynomial that fits the data distribution properly.

Sometimes, modelers operate under the mistaken belief that an approximation is acceptable because the data evens out in the end, so the results are not affected. That is not the case! Errors from the distribution data set can be compounded across multiple processes and the validity and confidence factor of the model are affected.

Although the team may have collected additional data points such as changeover and failure rates, it is important to hold off on inputting that portion of the data at this point.

APPLYING FLOW CONSTRAINTS IN MANUFACTURING

Flow constraints determine buffers, capacities, transfer of entities throughout the model, and any constraint that is related to how products flow. Applying these constraints can be an extensive endeavor and changes need to be made slowly and validated often.

A manufacturing environment contains a large number of constraints. Some of those constraints overlap with **warehousing** and **healthcare**, while others are unique to the **manufacturing** setting. Still, the **manufacturing** industry is a good starting point to examine the application of flow constraints because many of these constraints can also be found in other industries.

Before proceeding further, it is worthwhile to note that a high mix **manufacturing** operation and an **emergency department** in a hospital can both be represented with similar models. Both environments have an unknown and variable type of entities to process, arriving at unpredictable times, following variable routings, and all of those entities must be processed effectively. Whether the entity is a person or an order is not relevant from a process analysis point of view; the only difference is that in a **healthcare setting** the patient (the entity) needs to have a positive experience, whereas in **manufacturing** the customer must receive the order on time and within specs.

The following are some key constraints that need to be defined and the order in which they should be entered:

Process capacities, which represent the number of entities that can be processed at the same time. Entities may have the same or different VAT, but all entities are processed within the same constraints. Examples would be a paint line, an oven, or any other piece of equipment that can hold and process multiple items at a time.

Process buffers or in-process buffers, which represent any buffer available at the process step. Note that process buffers do not include accumulation conveyor capacities or any entity that is stored outside of the process area. **In-process buffers** consist of entities that are processed next at that station but are not stored in any other model entity.

Actual buffer locations within the operation. Each buffer location identified by a process must be defined without any VAT. Some buffers may require non-VAT to be defined in order to identify time to store and retrieve the entities. When setting up such buffers, it is important to identify the time required to store or retrieve the item as non-VAT. In all other cases, the buffer process should have no set timings associated with it.

Entity relationships, which should be defined and mapped out. Any assembly item consisting of multiple subassemblies or involving entity containment needs to be defined as well. An example could be a "multiple items per box, multiple boxes per pallet" relationship along with constraints on whether a pallet may have mixed boxes. Identifying these relationships is critical to the success of the model. The same applies to subassemblies, the number required, and their containment in the overall assembly process.

Subassemblies may also be defined as multiple levels of assemblies. The team must define all levels of subassemblies that are relevant to the model behavior and goal. Subassemblies should not be expanded if their production sequence does not impact the overall flow or results as defined in the goal-setting stage.

Material transfer, which includes all conveying equipment, material handling, and material transport relevant to the model. It is important not to include material movement that has no impact on the model behavior. For example, if the model assumes an unlimited supply of raw material, then adding the transfer and creation of raw material into the model has no effect on the results and should not be implemented.

When **setting up conveyors**, all settings for the conveyors need to be identified, including its speeds, dimensions, spacing between entities, accumulation behavior, and any other relevant settings. Acceleration and deceleration of the conveyor is important if it is not captured by the transfer rate of the entity and if it requires more than one time unit to achieve required speed. For example, if the time unit resolution of the model is one second, and the conveyor achieves required speeds within 0.5 seconds, then acceleration and deceleration may be ignored.

Other required material handling equipment should also be defined to include the time it takes to load and unload each item and time to transfer. Different pieces of material handling equipment may travel at different speeds depending on their loads and may require special handling that impacts the model results.

An automatic guided vehicle (AGV) or single track vehicle (STV) would be an example of material handling equipment with different behavior based on its environment. Each unit may need to be charged, may have different discharge rates based on load, may require intersection monitoring to avoid collision, and may travel at different speeds during the operation.

TRANSFERS AND ENTITY MOVEMENT BETWEEN STATIONS.

Entities cannot move instantaneously from one station to another in the real world; at least not yet. In order to make the simulation as accurate as possible:

- It is important to indicate that transfers exist,
- Have a cycle time associated with them, and
- Are required for the final product completion.

The entity transition can be based on either a speed/distance combination or a straight cycle time implementation depending on the environment and type of collected data.

APPLYING FLOW CONSTRAINTS IN HEALTHCARE

In a **healthcare setting**, the implementation of the processes can vary based on their designation. A bed, for example, does not have an in-process buffer, and patients cannot travel to the bed if it is occupied. Therefore, the bed capacity is always **one** and its buffer is always **zero**, regardless of whether there is one bed in a room or multiple.

The room is a collection of one or more beds, and it therefore contains one or more patients based on the number of beds. This concept applies to clinics, emergency rooms, operating rooms, hospital wings, and so on. There is always a one-to-one relationship between the bed and the patient.

A bed process undergoes multiple treatment cycles based on the patient condition. In the case where a simple capacity model is needed, the bed cycle time consists of the patient treatment time represented either as a distribution or from an imported data set. Each bed also requires a corresponding cleaning cycle that is applied after the patient leaves, so a cleaning entity must be present and tracked in order to properly simulate a healthcare setting.

Note that, at this point, there is no mention of providers. Resources need to be applied after the base model is built and validated. Incorporating the various aspects of the model in this order helps to simplify initial model creation and flow definition.

Patient transition and movement is another key aspect of a healthcare model. Patients transition from one location to another, sometimes with the aid of a provider to be entered later, and have transition distance and time associated with their transfer.

When elevators are required, elevator delays must be included in the model. Aisles and pathways need to identify the areas in which a patient is allowed to walk or transition. In some cases, multiple patients may be transported in an aisle, where in others a single patient is allowed to transfer. The model must include those key constraints in order to maintain its accuracy. Another crucial component of healthcare is the patient treatment cycle. When the patient is in a bed, the patient receives treatment from multiple providers, nurses, physicians, labs, and others. These providers walk to the bed, perform one or more process steps, and then proceed to another patient.

Those activities need to be captured based on the patient acuity and treatment so that proper cycle time and length of stay can be computed for each patient. The treatment process flow represents the potential process steps that are required to treat the patient. Some require one or more providers to be present, while others do not require any providers. Identifying the treatment cycle is key to proper expansion of healthcare models and is required for accurate representation of the current state.

Another aspect of the patient treatment cycle is the ability for the patient to leave the bed (sometimes with the help of a transport aid or provider), perform a task such as physical therapy or receiving an MRI, and then return to the same bed. The initially-allocated bed needs to be reserved for the same patient and may not be assigned to others. This behavior must be recognized and implemented at this step.

Software tools vary in their implementation of the treatment cycle. Some rely on code, some ignore it, and others include it as part of the model development environment. Any healthcare simulation tool that does not include a treatment cycle definition is limited or requires a lot of coding in order to implement the proper behavior.

APPLYING FLOW CONSTRAINTS IN WAREHOUSING

A **warehousing model** includes some steps from the manufacturing and healthcare modeling environments, plus key components that must be defined. The warehouse receives orders that need to be processed, contain some type of automation or material handling equipment, require space allocation for the entities, and contain multiple sections that have to interact. Creating a detailed warehouse simulation that contains all the racking and automation of the real-world site is key to proper modeling and getting the best results from the team's effort.

The first concept that comes to mind when people think of a "warehouse" is that of a large distribution center and it must handle a large volume of items. However, in reality, every operation has a warehousing component. For example, a treatment unit in a **hospital** has a small storage area that contains supplies and medications. That storage system has a picking operation, requires replenishment, needs to be slotted correctly, and has a put-away requirement. Similarly, in **manufacturing**, large buffers within the operation are stored in a warehouse-like setting that requires the same set of activities. **Warehousing** simulations are therefore useful for many different operations, not only for the traditional distribution center.

A warehouse is made up of three main areas:

1. The receiving and pre-storage area,
2. The shipping and order staging area, and
3. The storage area where items are stored, picked or replenished based on need.

Therefore, when defining the warehouse, each of these locations needs to be taken into account. Depending on the requirements of the model, some areas may not need to be expanded to include the full detail.

By following the product flow in the warehouse, receiving and pre-storage is the first section where items are introduced into the warehouse. This section can be defined by two factors: 1) the quantities and schedule of items being received and 2) the requirement constraints on the size and variability of items received. The quantities and schedules are defined by the arrival and delivery schedule to the warehouse including the containment of the items being received. This includes pallet sizing, arrival delays, delivery content and others. The "other" aspect represents any processing that needs to be performed on the received items before they are stored, which includes re-packaging, sorting, re-palletizing and any additional processing required in order to properly store the items in logical and effective way.

When additional processing is required after receiving, additional data is required to identify volume and time required in order to properly identify the flow. The section may need to be expanded if it impacts the flow of pallets to the storage area and has the potential to introduce congestion.

Storage and picking areas normally constitute the area warehouse section that can provide extensive ROI on the implementation. Storage consists of moving items from the initial staging area to storage racks, and picking consists of all activities required to convert the received items into customer orders. Although storage is less complex than picking, it deals with item containers and pallets. This can still have its own set of challenges especially when replenishment and storage generate aisle congestion and location contention.

In the **picking area**, orders might be split into multiple pick sequences and have to be staged before they are ready to ship. Therefore, the model needs to:

- Expand the data set required for the pick orders,
- Define how it is to be loaded into the model, and
- Build the required infrastructure in the model to support either the data import or the random creation of the order set.

At minimum, each order sequence should contain the number of items of each type that need to be picked and the item type identifiers. The staging area needs to be expanded to include any potential order sequencing needed to support the picking cycle, including the constraint of order splitting across multiple carts when needed.

Staging and shipping is the third component of the warehouse and is responsible for grouping the orders, organizing truck loading, and perform all required shipping information. In some cases, a sortation system is introduced into the staging area in order to help group the orders together. In order to support staging, an item definition set needs to be present. A simple warehouse model may be based only on distributions of item locations, weight, dimensions, and so on. A detailed and more accurate representation loads the actual information of the products being stored, including their location, size, weight and any additional special handling information that may be required. This information is often found in the WMS. By optimizing the location of each item with respect to the pick cycle, pick path, and congestion analysis, the warehouse can gain efficiency and reduce its operational cost.

The data set may be stored inside the model or referenced through a direct connection to an external data set, but the modeling tool in use must not impose any size constraint on how large the data set may be. Any limitation on the size of the data imposes a limitation on the model analysis later on. Therefore, the minimum data set for proper implementation should include location definition, whether that consists of racks, Automated Storage and Retrieval Systems (ASRS), floor space or any other storage for the items.

Item definition constraints such as volume, weight, items per box, and boxes per pallet may be required at a later stage of the model building process. This data is necessary for detailed analysis mainly to replace the approximation of distributions.

The model developer should include provisions for such data sets to be imported into the model.

Staging areas need to be defined and any spatial constraint needs to be identified early on in the model-building cycle. Information about unmovable constraints, structure limitations, and path constraints should be collected. Some constraints may not pertain directly to the process, but they may impact the optimization path of the distribution center.

Last but not least, are the resources or man-power available to perform the tasks? These include the number and type of resources available, efficiencies, and shifts. Picking limitations also need to be collected. Limitations of this nature might consist of maximum items per pick sequence, multiple pick requirements, and weight constraints.

From a pure picking perspective, picking methods are important in identifying the efficiency of the distribution center. This information is normally available in the WMS (or equivalent) and includes the wave picking requirement, maximum items per pick, and pick path.

In the case of a new warehouse/distribution center analysis, the pick sequences and constraints are identified by the model. General assumptions can be made early on and finalized after the model is completed. Assumptions need to be realistic and should allow the modeler to quickly modify them without impacting the model definition. These assumptions might include cache speed of the picker, maximum weight of the pick cart, and number or size of waves.

RECAP

Of course, every operation has its own unique challenges and constraints. The definitions in this chapter serve as a foundation, but later chapters describe industry-specific implementation in greater detail.

It is important to remember that the goal of model-building is to create an accurate, efficient, functional simulation, not merely a visually appealing one. More than aesthetically pleasing graphics, what matters is the model's behavior under different constraints so that the simulation can be as useful as possible.

Chapter 7 discusses methods of expanding a basic model into an advanced model that is more complex and detailed. Therefore it is truer to life than a basic model may be.

Once the necessary constraints are fully integrated and validated, the model as a whole needs to be validated with different data sets. This robust historical data ensures that all conditions are accounted for and that the model is representative of the live environment. This final validation is discussed in Chapter 8: Model Validation.

Chapter 7: Expanding the Model and Adding Detail

The completion of a basic model is a considerable milestone. However, once the initial details are implemented and validated, it can be difficult to identify how much more detail to add.

After the initial model-building efforts are complete, the developer should return to the original goal of the simulation model and use this goal to determine the amount of detail to add. It is imperative at this point to plan properly so that the model includes only important information and is not cluttered up with unwanted details.

As discussed earlier, there should be a clear distinction between simulation for analysis and visualization of the flow. Simulation for analysis and optimization generates the most ROI, while visualization is important to display the system flow.

At this time, the developer should also consider any potential model expansions that may take place in the future. It is important to build the model so that it can be properly expanded without impacting the completed portions. Failure to implement proper planning for model expansion reduces the ROI of the model development as well as the effectiveness and usefulness of the model.

This task differentiates the experienced modeler from the novice. A novice might add too much unnecessary detail or fail to build the proper hooks for future expansion into the model; in advance. An experienced modeler introduces specific processes that can be expanded in the future without impacting the current analytical goal set.

After some general remarks on different types of simulation tools, this chapter introduces **three examples** of how to create a model that achieves present goals while preparing for future expansion.

<u>CHOOSING A SIMULATION TOOL</u>

Once again, the type of simulation tool that a team chooses to utilize can be the difference between a timely, effective simulation and a stressful project that drags on indefinitely.

While some simulation tools recognize that not every modeling team member is an experienced developer—and that many people use simulation as only *part* of their jobs, not their whole job—other tools are not as user-friendly. Some tools use old technologies that have been retrofit to run on current hardware. Others are simply designed for students in an educational market, which involves very different goals from the professional workplace.

Oftentimes, the types of simulation projects assigned in **educational environments** are not practical in an industry setting. A student may be required to complete one or two models in a semester; a basic capacity model for an emergency department might take four months. This timeline is unacceptable in the workplace, as the current state of the operation changes over those months and would render the model unusable—and certainly unable to be expanded if the original goals changed.

While the technology used in an educational setting may be suitable for this kind of months-long project, it does not meet the standards of an industry professional.

Industry-based simulation tools, in contrast, provide an abundance of easier methods to expand the models even in cases without proper goal planning. Such tools utilize simulation engines that are not based on code, but instead include specific features that allow quick modifications to the environment. These modifications can take place through a simple routing change or a detailed sub-flow expanding the functionality of the processes.

These advanced tools can cut down the model development time from months to a few days or weeks. Because the model is created in a timely fashion, it can actually be used for analysis before it becomes obsolete due to changes in the work environment.

Companies must make careful, informed choices when it comes to simulation software. Many models fail to provide any meaningful analysis due to the complexity of the tool being used. To salvage their efforts, companies opt for a visually-pleasing 3D environment, replacing substantive analysis with a "wow" factor in order to save face after an ineffective modeling project.

Most useful models do have decent 2D or 3D representation capabilities, but more importantly, they contain the proper logic required to perform meaningful analysis and provide sound recommendations. It is more important for a team to question the validity of a model than the attractiveness of its displays. Model validators and analysis recipients need to be aware of what actually matters in order to determine whether a model is trustworthy and complete.

HYPOTHETICAL CASE: HEALTHCARE

A **surgical center** can be used as an example of a model that is designed to analyze current goals but can be expanded to answer new questions in the future. The basic model, developed according to the process described in the previous chapter, would have all operating rooms, paths, and hallways defined. Pre-op and post-op locations would be identified and implemented, resources would be defined, and a schedule would be set up and loaded into the model. At this point, the modelers must examine whether or not this model achieves their current goal.

For the sake of example, the present goal is to identify the capacity of the department with and without resource constraints. Some future goals eventually are to identify the sequence of surgical cart supplies to the rooms and their corresponding cleaning and replenishment activities. Determine optimal location for gurneys and temporary storage. And to determine if it is feasible to combine pre- and post-op into the same area.

Therefore, although the model is initially developed as a capacity model, it needs to have the proper hooks so that it can be expanded without affecting the initial implementation.

In this particular case, a surgical patient would be unable to proceed with the surgery until the surgical cart(s) are available next to the surgical room. Therefore the initial model may be implemented with the surgical cart requirement built in, including the wait for the cart(s) to be available. However, it should be set up with an unlimited supply of carts that are always present when needed.

In doing so, the cart availability constraint does not affect the initial model, but future investigations about cart supply impact can take place with only a few simple modifications.

In addition, when the surgery is complete, and as the patient exits the room, a set of dirty carts should be released from the room and sent to a generic location without any constraints. This setup does not affect the model at present, but allows for future demand in the supply chain of carts to occur.

By tying the type of surgery performed to the number of carts consumed or generated, a much better environment for expansion is developed. This choice ensures that the expanded model is valid and can be analyzed quickly.

All of these strategies create a model that serves its initial goal *and* provide answers to questions that arise in the future. By planning for future expansion during the creation of the initial model, developers save themselves a significant amount of effort down the line.

HYPOTHETICAL CASE: DISTRIBUTION CENTER

Although the above example is a healthcare model, the same concept applies to warehouses, supply chain, manufacturing, automation, office flow, and others.

Consider a **distribution center (DC) model** in which the original goal is to optimize picking capacity and methods. The model must be implemented with the future in mind so that the team can eventually improve replenishment patterns, slotting, receiving, racking allocation, and manpower allocation, as well as expanding staging and shipping. The original model must allow the team to study the impact of any changes in these areas.

Normally, in a DC implementation, the model progresses to different areas in order to properly study the impact of improvement throughout the facility. The model for the DC must be built with the expansion in mind, without adding too many details and rendering the simulation too complex to be useful.

At the front end of the DC model, a basic workflow should be set up for the receiving area that is unconstrained with unlimited capacity. A pallet storage area should also be created with no constraints on the area's size or capacity. The replenishment logic should be minimal unless replenishment and picking follow the same path.

The replenishment path may become a critical path if replenishment is performed at the same time as picking, or if the two processes share resources or paths. If neither constraint is present, replenishment paths may be set up but not used at this point.

Note that the simulation tools should be able to provide a quick way to create the paths. If creating paths is a time-consuming factor for any of the moving entities, then the modeling tool is not appropriately suited for the implementation.

Shipping and staging areas also need to be set up. Like the receiving and storage areas, they should have unlimited capacities and no constraints on dock doors and truck availability. The workflow is used later on to analyze the changes in the picking area to the staging and shipping area.

Both pre- and post-picking workflow need to be entered in order to expand the DC model and reuse it for future analysis. The expanded flow also helps when presenting the model, as it provides a complete view of the operation instead of merely a segment of the DC.

As with the healthcare model, having a tool that allows for simplified model expansion without impacting the existing and validated model is a plus. This capability reduces model development time and facilitates faster access to analysis, both of which are imperative to increase simulation ROI.

Like healthcare and warehouse models, **manufacturing models** must be built with expansion in mind, yet avoid overcomplicating the model.

Consider an assembly line production environment with parts assembled onto a main unit as it progresses through the flow. Some stations within the line have a unique, specific cycle time, while others are designed to perform additional operations on the part such as QA or other value-added processes.

The initial goal of the simulation effort may be to load level the line and reduce any non-VAT in the overall process. A future goal may be to identify Kanban sizes of all sub-components feeding the line, expand the sub-assembly delivery processes, and expand the manufacturing processes.

Just like the healthcare setting with its unlimited supply of surgical carts, the manufacturing model should be built with its assembly operations present, but with a basic workflow process that delivers an unlimited supply of parts.

The main line can be load leveled and analyzed independently of the subassembly component delivery, Kanban size, and any other factor related to the sub-component availability. Then, when the model has been further analyzed and validated, each sub-component implementation can be easily expanded without impacting the validity of the main line.

HOW MUCH DETAIL TO ADD

In short, enough detail must be added to analyze and complete the goal of the simulation. If additional details do not impact the current goal or provide a basic hook to allow for a future expansion, they are a waste of time in the overall implementation process.

It is important for the modeling team members to be ready to defend their choices to omit particular details. Stakeholders often suggests that specific details need to be added due to notable recent events, but developers must remain thoughtful and deliberate with their choices.

For example, a piece of equipment may have been experiencing excessive downtime that, when properly repaired, eliminates the resulting delay. The stakeholders may insist that this detail should be included as a constraint. Modelers should know that this situation is better suited to be run as a scenario for analysis and not as part of the model constraint. Therefore, the model developer must be able to provide the proper explanation to the stakeholders and make sound decisions regarding the content of the model.

After the first implementation of the model, certain processes may need to be expanded in order to make the model more complete. This operation normally occurs after the initial goal is accomplished and further analysis is desired.

Since the model was built with this expansion in mind (or a proper tool was used to minimize the impact of the expansion on the original model), it is certainly possible to add details to the model by including more relevant information later down the line. There are two main methods of including more detail: 1) expanding specific processes in the main model, or 2) expanding the model through internal sub-flows.

In the first option, where the model is expanded within the canvas or section, the initial model may become more complicated. This increased complexity can make it more difficult to quickly disconnect from the expanding flow.

In the second option, the process that was implemented in the initial model is converted in a sub-flow operation. As objects or entities enter the process, their true process flow is defined based on a separate sub-flow that is implemented as a side operation. This option has many benefits, including the ability to have multiple developers work on individual sub-flows that can be merged together in the overall model.

Image 7-1 illustrates a simple sub-flow.

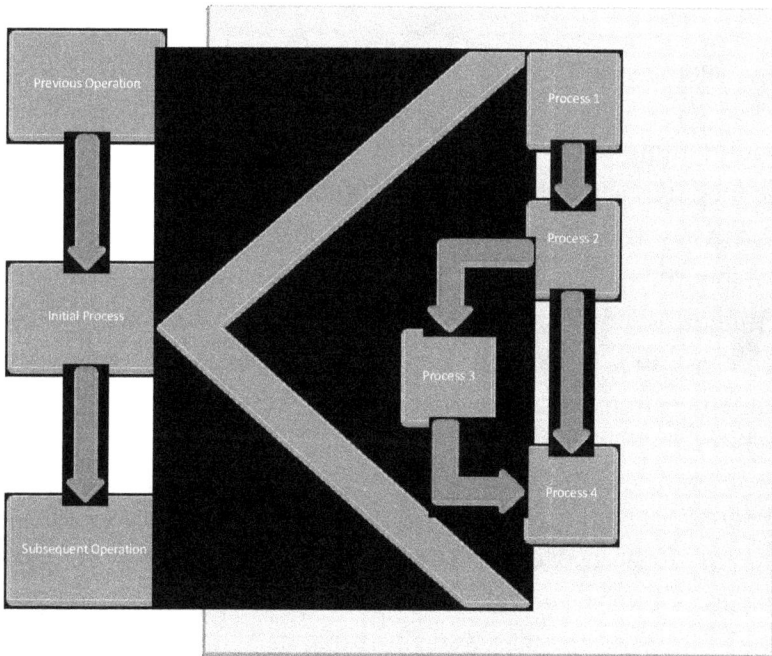

Image 7-1. Example of a sub-flow.

As objects or entities enter the initial process, they are automatically transitioned to Process One in the sub-flow process. Each entity proceeds through the sub-flow until it is ready to complete the operation at the end of the initial process. The sub-flow may be different based on the entity or object type, and may require different constraints.

One of the advantages of sub-flows is that they can be completely implemented and validated outside of the main model. The only requirement is to maintain the proper naming convention for the objects and constraints in order to simplify the merge into the main model. Another advantage provided by the use of sub-flows is the ability to quickly disconnect the sub-flow when needed and switch back to a simple cycle time operation. For complex models, sub-flows greatly simplify the model development cycle, allowing the model creation and validation process to occur more efficiently.

RESOURCE CONSTRAINTS

Incorporating resource constraints is an important step in making the model as accurate as it needs to be. Resources might include an orderly transferring patients, a picker or replenisher in a warehouse, or an assembly line worker in a manufacturing setting. Resources are not limited to people: an automatic guided vehicle, a fork truck, a gurney, and any other entity required to process or transfer an object can all be considered resources as well.

Resources are normally constraints that impose limits on the process flow because processes may require one or more resources in order to take place. Resources are associated with availability, efficiencies, and shifts that need to be defined. They may have travel time associated with their empty travel (traveling without an entity to perform an operation). Certain resources, especially the ones representing people, can have diminishing efficiency factors related to fatigue, which may impact the overall throughput of the system.

The following are three examples of how resource constraints might be added to models from different industries.

In **healthcare**, an operating department capacity analysis implementation may start as single processes for each of the operating rooms, along with pre- and post-op processes. The team adds a set for hallways identifying patient flow within the department and basic resource constraints. Developers also load different data sets and apply surgery-type distributions and schedules, so the model is sufficient to generate capacity constraints, identify bottlenecks, and perform minor schedule improvement and pre/post-op optimization.

This is the basic model. In order to expand this model, the team should expand each operating room to support the details of the process flow. Availability of resources (surgical nurses, surgeons, anesthesiologists, and so on) should be introduced in the model. Surgical carts and their cleaning cycle must be implemented and expanded along with the cleaning cycles of the room.

A model with these expansions provides much more analysis and a more accurate representation of the current flow. It also helps with scheduling by identifying the most efficient breakdown of room allocation by surgery type, number of completed surgeries, cost information, the load on the staff, and surgical cart requirements.

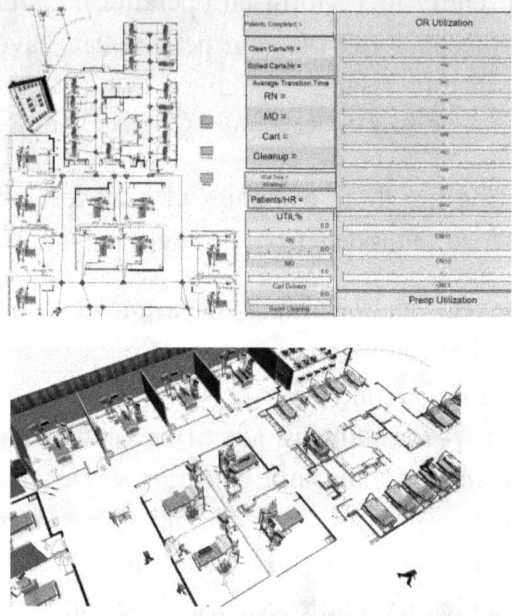

Image 7-2. 2D and 3D represenation of a sample healthcare model.

In a **manufacturing environment**, proper model implementation helps in expanding the model to include all constraints within the environment. By progressively expanding and validating the model, it is possible to generate one simulation environment that encompasses all aspects of the manufacturing facility, from raw material to the final project ready for shipment.

Note that when building the model, it is always simpler and faster to start with large building blocks, then expand each one into the required detail to support the goal. In contrast, starting from a cell and expanding outwards generates a lot of model changes that require extensive and repeated validation, which wastes precious time that is better used for analysis and optimization.

121

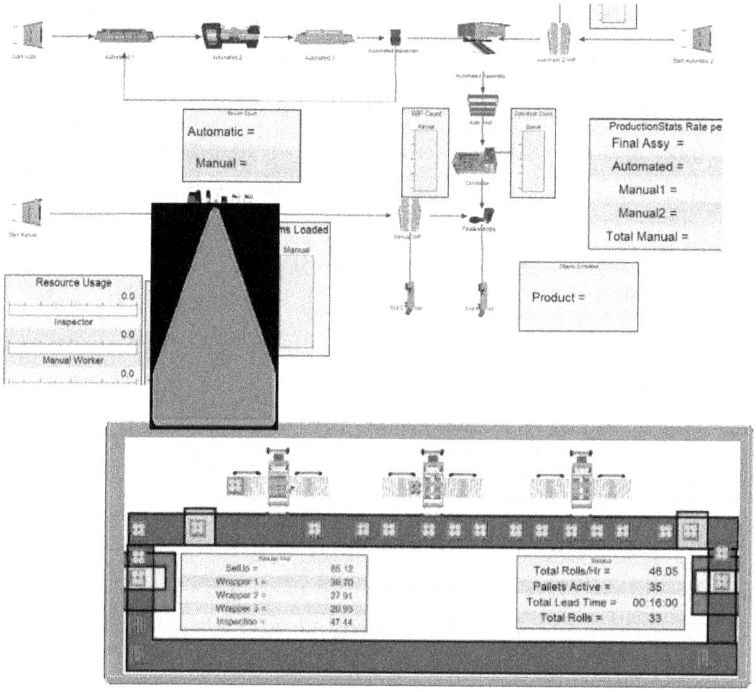

Image 7-3. A manufacturing simulation with sub-flows.

Warehouses and distribution center models can also benefit from planning ahead for future expansion. There are many elements to consider, including pickers, staff running the fork truck, the rate of replenishment into the pick areas, and so on. All of these processes run at different shifts and have different constraints that should be included in the model.

For example, consider an operation such as an online store, in which orders come in for multiple items to be sent to a single address. These items must first be picked and then assembled and packaged in a staging area before they are sent off to the shipping area.

Imagine that the staging area staff work more quickly than the pickers, sending multi-item orders to the staging area before they have been fully assembled. A three-item order might be shipped out in two or three separate packages rather than all three items being sent in one, just because the pickers were unable to match the pace of the staging area staff. Shipping costs increase significantly because the picking and staging areas are out of sync.

It is therefore important for a modeler to include constraints regarding the different rates at which different portions of the warehouse process their items. The unique constraints of each area impact the whole operation and must be fully considered in order to increase efficiency.

Another key point to remember when expanding warehouse models is that employees must do a large amount of walking to get from place to place. This travel time adds up and affects the overall flow of the operation, so it must also be incorporated into the model.

RECAP

This chapter discussed a number of practical concerns regarding model expansion, including important considerations when choosing a simulation tool. Several examples illustrated how basic models in different industries might be expanded to include more detail.

After the models are developed, they need to be validated in order to make sure that they represent the actual environment they mimic. The validation process must be performed before each and every analysis step and before any model recommendation is generated. A complete validation should also be performed after every significant set of changes is added to the model. The next chapter discusses the validation process in greater detail.

Chapter 8: Model Validation

Simulations are as varied as the tasks they set out to model, but there is one thing they all have in common: they must be validated.

A valid simulation matches reality as closely as is necessary for the simulation to be useful. Validation, then, compares simulation outcomes and analytics to data from the real-world process on which the simulation is based.

An important difference to note early in the validation process is the distinction between validation and verification. **Verification** means making sure the model matches its intended specifications—ensuring that the simulation developers have done what they planned to do. **Validation** looks at the simulation and compares it to the real world, ensuring that the *simulation itself* does what it was intended to do.[31]

While it is nearly impossible to recreate reality perfectly, simulations must come close enough to predict future events with a reasonable degree of confidence. The specifics of that degree of confidence depends on the type of simulation, what it is used for, and other contextual details, but the overall principle remains the same. If a simulation cannot consistently replicate the real circumstances and environment on which it is based, it is useless.

Visually appealing animated models are often susceptible to this kind of flaw. It can be hard to spot inaccuracies in a model that is engaging and pleasing to the eye. It is important to remember

---

[31] John S. Carson, "Model Verification and Validation," *Proceedings of the 2002 Winter Simulation Conference* (2002), accessed June 5, 2017, http://informs-sim.org/wsc02papers/008.pdf.

that without validity, these animated models are just smoke and mirrors without the substance that would make them useful.

Animations are not inherently bad; on the contrary. Sometimes the very goal of a simulation is to visualize a process that can be hard to understand without animation or imagery. (If that is the case, this goal should have been outlined during the goal-setting stage.) If the goal is visualization rather than analysis, an animation tool can be sufficient to meet the team's needs; as long as that animated process can still be validated effectively. Validation is always a critical step in every simulation.

If both visualization and analysis are important to a simulation's outcome, it can be helpful to perform the detailed animation in a different setting than the analysis model. That way, the analysis model can retain the general animation without getting cluttered up with tiny details. The team can avoid wasting analysis time on animation and vice versa. If the models are divided up, each one can focus directly on a specific goal; animation or analysis. Each one can be validated based on the needs of that type of simulation.

Adapting the validation process to fit the needs of every simulation project leads to the most efficient and accurate results. A one-size-fits-all list of validation tests may waste time while failing to examine the main process closely enough.

For example, in the case of a **manufacturing** facility, there might be different standards of accuracy for different parts of the simulation. Some aspects of the model might need to meet very strict validation standards, such as cycle times or lead times. On the other hand, animation quality or details regarding operations outside of the main process flow can often afford to be held to slightly less rigid standards without compromising model integrity.

With that in mind, the team should build and validate a model that is pertinent to the task to be analyzed. Members must understand which details have a significant impact on analysis and which have not. Expanding the model detail to encompass unnecessary areas leads to longer development times. More extensive validation efforts. And increased data requirements for proper analysis. In short, to more work for less benefit.

<u>PRIORITIZING THE MAIN PROCESS</u>

RUNNING OUTLIERS AS WHAT-IF SCENARIOS

It is important at this point to identify the main process flow **validation cycle**. An event that rarely occurs within the flow should be considered as an independent scenario rather than putting the added constraints into the system.

The key is to identify the rogue conditions and define them as scenarios to run in the analysis phase. The law of diminishing returns comes into play in this environment, so the development team should identify the detail needed to effectively create a useful model.

Adding too much detail delays the development and validation cycle and provides little to no benefit to the analysis later on. The goal of a model is to be useful; a model that is never finished because of an endless series of tiny changes in peripheral details does not accomplish this goal.

When running the many different outlying scenarios with varying sets of constraints, it is important to ensure that the analytics of these scenarios do not bleed together. The analytics should cover only one scenario at a time rather than taking averages and making predictions based off of many combined what-if cases. These scenarios all take place under uncommon conditions; combining these unusual circumstances into an average does not provide useful results.

It is best to have a model that can remain in a steady state as these changes in constraints are made. In interactive modeling environments, changes can be implemented and examined right away because the modeling and simulation engine are in sync. User interaction can be passed dynamically to the engine while the simulation is running. Thereby providing immediate feedback to the user. Note that in interactive modeling environments, the simulator needs to be able to manage the analysis data set. And allow the user to test the analysis data as needed.

Advantages of Interactive Models

A common error that teams commit when building a simulation is to wait until the model is fully built before beginning to validate. If testing is done on the entire system rather than on its component parts and an error is found, it can be difficult to isolate the source of the error. In addition, testing only on the system as a whole can actually hide existing issues in cases of error cancellation.

Circumventing this problem is as simple as validating earlier and more often. The optimum method of validation is to check the behavior as the model is being built, preferably while the simulation is running.

For these reasons, it is very important to make sure that the component parts and the interfaces between them are tested in addition to the system as a whole.[32] Interactive simulation software can be a great tool to help with this task.

In interactive simulations, constraints and definitions can be changed during the simulation run with direct effect on the running simulation. This immediate adaptation allows validation of each component to occur every step of the way, even while the changes are being made. Users can detect and fix errors as they arise in individual sections of the model rather than waiting until the end to search the whole simulation for inaccuracies.

As an example, changing routing behavior, timing properties, and other constraints while the simulation is running allows for immediate validation of those changes without restarting the model each time. Moreover, since the model is reacting in real time to the user interaction, it is possible to introduce boundary conditions and test each behavior, one constraint at a time, without compromising model integrity or slowing down development time.

Interactive simulation validation can bear some similarities to multi-player video games. In a gaming environment, feedback from the user action is immediate, and other actors and entities in the game react to it as it occurs. The best simulation models, like video games, react to changes in real time and provide instant feedback.

---

[32] Ben H. Thacker et al., "Concepts of Model Verification and Validation," *Los Alamos National Laboratory*, accessed June 5, 2017, http://www.ltas-vis.ulg.ac.be/cmsms/uploads/File/LosAlamos_VerificationValidation.pdf.

Because interactive simulation allows validation to happen continuously, there is a smaller chance of discovering validation issues at the end of the model development cycle. In fact, model development and validation time may be reduced by up to 50%. This time is saved because validation occurs continuously, without restarting the model each time, and is provided in real-time on the interface. Transition to the analysis phase occurs much more quickly as a result of this saved time.

CONTINUOUS VALIDATION AND FINAL VALIDATION

In the creation of a model, each new addition should be validated. This **continuous validation** prevents errors from building up and makes them easier to spot and fix when they arise. But if that validation takes place all throughout the model-building process, what tests are necessary during the final model validation phase?

Certain aspects of the model are best tested continuously, and other aspects are best tested after the model is built. Sometimes the validation that occurs after the model is built catches mistakes that could not be identified earlier. For this reason, it is important to test during *and* after model creation.

During model-building, tests were run with a set of sample data. Errors were caught and corrections were made within the context of that small sample size. Now, in **final validation**, tests should use more extensive historical data as opposed to a sample from only a few days. This variation can help to ensure that the model is equipped to handle the full complexity of real-life data, not just a sample used to represent it.

Another attribute unique to the final model validation step is that **Monte Carlo** runs are performed. This process is explained in more detail later in the chapter. Monte Carlo runs are designed to consider the extent of variability and determine how useful the simulation is. If there is too much variability, the final model validation step pinpoints the source of the variation so the modeling team can address it.

Continuous validation is a critical component of successful simulation-building, but a final set of tests during the **post-construction validation** phase can help to catch errors in the model as a whole. Tests like Monte Carlo runs are most effective once the model is fully built, and the model can be examined with a more extensive data set once all model components are in place.

THE VALIDATION PROCESS

Validation can include many kinds of tests on each part of the model, as well as on the model as a whole. Different people can test the model in different ways; many options are available depending on a team's resources and priorities.

The team who developed the model can test it, since its members are most knowledgeable about what the simulation is capable of accomplishing. Those who are using the model can also test it, since it was created for their benefit. An independent third party can conduct the examination for reasons of impartiality, or—less effectively—a scoring model can be used to see how the simulation measures up to objective criteria.[33]

Those who are chosen to test the model, whoever they may be, have a substantial arsenal of techniques available to them. They could examine **face validity**, for example, by asking experts in

---

[33] Robert G. Sargent, "Verification and Validation of Simulation Models," *Proceedings of the 2011 Winter Simulation Conference* (2011). Accessed May 31, 2017, http://www.informs-sim.org/wsc11papers/016.pdf.

the field whether the simulation seems reasonable and if its results make sense.[34] This type of validity testing is one of the briefest and easiest, since it requires only a cursory examination of the simulation. It is often insufficient to determine model validity on its own; it is best used in conjunction with other types of testing.

Another potential test is that of **event validity**, which considers whether the events in the simulation match the events in real life. One example of event validity testing would be to compare the number of appointment no-shows in real life and in the simulation to see if they are the same.[35] The team might also examine extreme conditions in order to make sure that the model handles outliers properly. Another option is to put the simulation through predictive validation, in which the simulation's predictions about future events are compared to how those events actually transpire.[36]

Those tests are some of the most common ones, but there are many more that can be used depending on the needs of the organization. With so many options, it can be hard to identify where to start. In what order should team members conduct this testing? What parts of the model should be tested first?

During model-building, the first step of continuous validation should be to validate the model flow. It is important to ensure that entities flow through the model in the same way that they do in the real-life process.

As the model is built, test each section individually.

---

[34] Ibid.

[35] Ibid.

[36] Ibid.

First, validate that section's flow. Do entities follow the same path that they do in real life? Do they move at the same speed? Do bottlenecks occur at the same places? Are the input and output of that part the same as its real-life counterpart?

Second, validate the connections between sections. When items pass from one work station to another, does it take the same amount of time as in reality? Correct any errors here before moving forward, as these inter-process connections can make a significant difference when it comes to total process time and throughput.

Once all the individual components are tested and their connections match the data, then it is time to validate the model as a whole. This is where "model validation" begins as its own step after model construction.

Ensure that objects flow through the entire model at the proper rate and that input, throughput, and output match the real-life data. Examine face validity. Test extreme conditions and outliers. Include a more extensive set of historical data. Now is the time to push the model to its limits in order to make sure that it matches the process it is meant to simulate.

While examining the model flow, the VSM made during the goal-setting stage can be a useful tool. Compare the simulation results to the process identified in the VSM and address any differences or discrepancies. Value stream mapping creates a detailed, step-by-step analysis of every aspect of a process, so it can be very helpful when checking each step of the model for accuracy. What's important in this step is the content of the VSM and not its visual representation. The model validator needs to look at the VAT, non-VAT, process and object efficiencies, process utilization, OEE and others. Those values can be represented in a report format, a visual representation, or an extended VSM.

Once this is complete, the model flow is essentially validated, and from there the team can move forward to more complicated tests if they are necessary. The nature of these tests depends on the purpose of the simulation, so they may vary widely. For example, one such test could use the model to predict the day's output based on that day's conditions, then examine the output at the end of the day to see if it matches.

Above all, testing should be tailored to the team's goals: does the model provide the information it was created to provide in a reliable and accurate manner? If the answer is no, this is the time to make changes.

THE MONTE CARLO METHOD

One technique to examine data variability is to use the **Monte Carlo method**. The Monte Carlo method runs thousands of possible scenarios and assigns them weight by likelihood, providing a full range of possibilities; best case scenario, worst case scenario, and thousands in between.

It works through the use of randomization. For every uncertain variable, random data within a defined range is used. Thousands of iterations later, the most probable outcomes are weighted more heavily, while the less likely scenarios (the outliers) fall to the sidelines. This type of analysis allows the person running it to understand what is likeliest to happen as well as to visualize the chances of very good and very bad outcomes.

When running a simulation, a team must consider the outliers, just as the Monte Carlo method includes information about the less likely (but often more extreme) outcomes. The team should prioritize on the most probable outcomes, since those are what's expected to occur the majority of the time.

Less probable circumstances should not be discounted. However, they should be run as scenarios. A simulation should be prepared for them. It should not treat them as the norm, or even as a likely event.

All of these mistakes may seem innocuous. Even small changes made to input accuracy can have profound effects on the output of a simulation. By making the minor adjustments necessary to avoid these simple errors, it is possible to improve a simulation's accuracy substantially.

Monte Carlo runs determine the extent of variability in the model. If the model is conforming, that is, reasonably consistent and useful for prediction purposes, it does not need alterations to its variability. In the case where the model is not conforming and its results are inconsistent and unpredictable, that model does not serve its purpose or make accurate predictions.

If a model is found to be non-conforming, the validation team can search through the different parts of the model to find the source of the extreme variability and attempt to correct the issue at its origin. It is rare that a model gets to this point without anyone having identified the issue of extreme variability. The test is nonetheless important to ensure that the model as a whole is useful and accurate.

The following six images provide examples of different levels of variability and conformity.

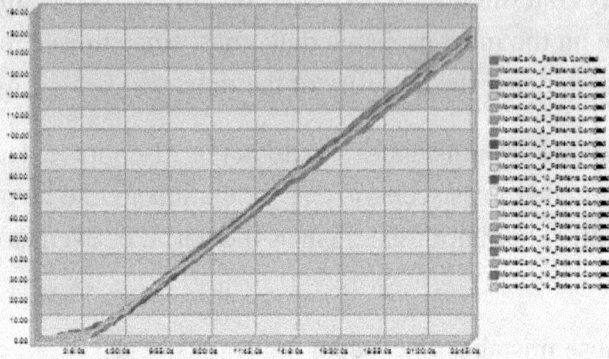

Image 8-1. Multiple runs and a conforming data set. Model variability does not affect simulation results in this case.

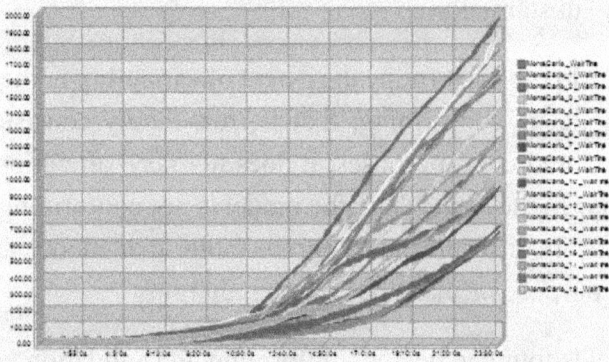

Image 8-2. Multiple runs with highly variable but trending results. This type of model may not be used for analysis except in Monte Carlo mode.

135

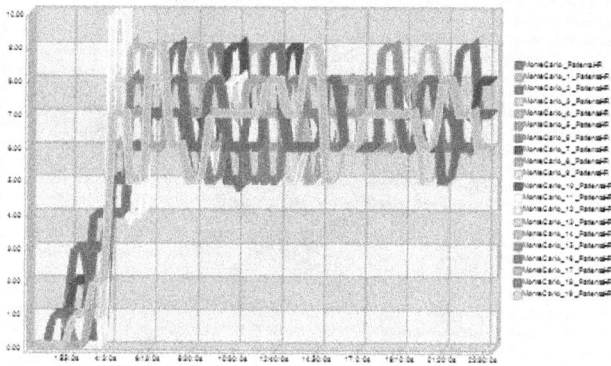

Image 8-3. This case exhibits high variability and an inconsistent output.

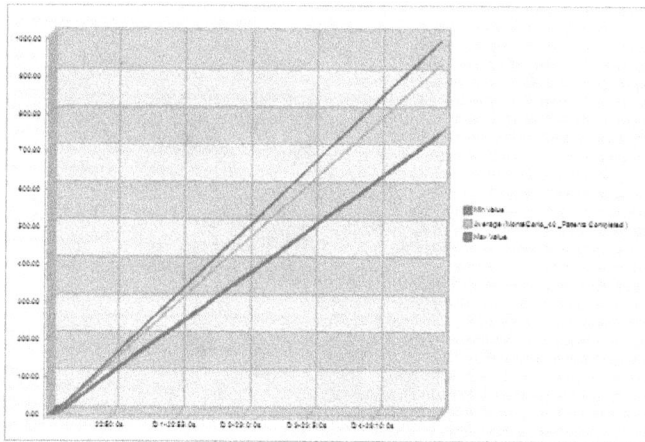

Image 8-4. Multiple runs viewed as Min/Max/Average. Model variability does not affect simulation results in this case.

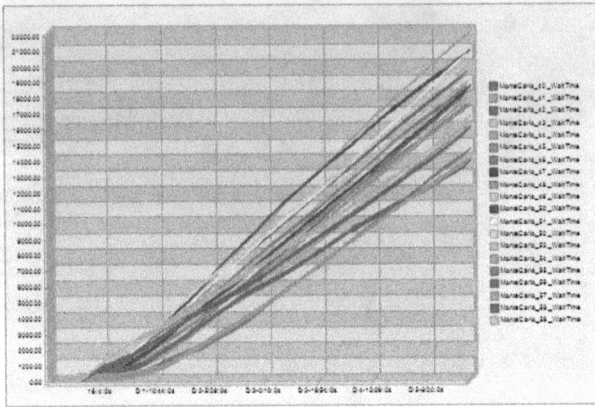

Image 8-5. Model variability with proper trending. These results should be interpreted with a lower confidence factor unless Monte Carlo simulation is used for new analysis.

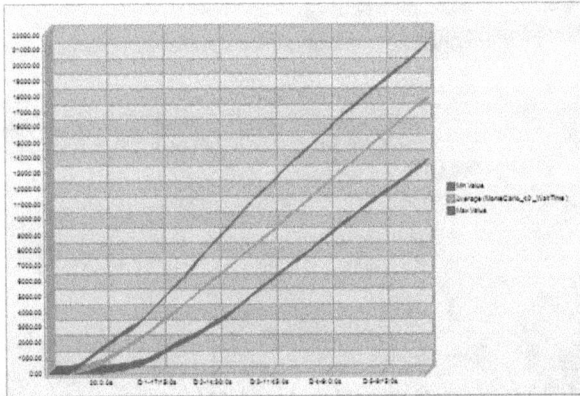

Image 8-6. Min/Max/Average for Image 8-5 showing variability factor.

RECAP

Model validation takes place throughout the model-building stage. Also as its own step after the model is fully constructed.

By validating during model-building, the team can catch small errors as they arise and prevent them from influencing other parts of the model.

By validating afterward, the team can identify full-model errors, issues of variability, and other concerns that may not be evident when looking only at subsections of the model. Tests of face and event validity, Monte Carlo runs, and use of full historical data can all provide greater insight into how the model performs under real-life conditions.

One component that can aid in validation is the use of an interactive simulation software. That is, the kind that can create a model that adapts to changes on the fly and can validate continuously rather than constantly needing to stop and rerun with each change. This type of software saves time and effort by allowing the model-building team to make changes without restarting the model with every alteration.

Using software that does not require the team to rewrite extensive amounts of code also saves time during this process and ensures that the model is validated effectively and intuitively, as painlessly as possible.

After the model is fully validated and all flaws have been minimized to an acceptable level or eliminated entirely, the simulation can be put to use for analysis.

Chapter 9: Basic Analysis and Metrics

After the model is built and validated, the analysis phase can begin. The "analysis" phase is actually divided into three components.

1. The team identifies and collects key metrics.
2. The team analyzes those metrics and the flow as a whole.
3. The team optimizes the simulation in order to generate a solution to the defined or detected problem set.

This chapter covers the first step by explaining how to identify what metrics to collect and how to go about collecting them. The next two steps are covered in the next chapter.

The image below depicts the progression of the analysis phase.

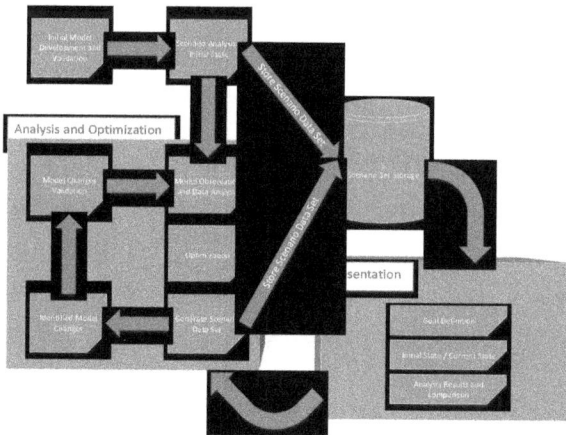

Image 9-1. Analysis, optimization, and presentation.

The analysis phase is the key reason for the project. It is time to use the model to gather information about the real-world processes it simulates and make decisions for improvement. The entire model development process culminates in the analysis phase, which ultimately determines the success or failure of the project. A model development project should allocate more time to analysis than to any other phase. Visibility, success, and ROI (the most important results of the project) are all determined at this time. It is imperative to reach this phase quickly in order to make the most out of the model.

Part of the reason that it is important to reach the analysis phase promptly is because analysis is where the benefits of the simulation-building process are reaped. Another reason to strive for timeliness in reaching this stage is that the workplace is a rapidly-changing environment. For a model to be useful, it must reach the analysis phase while it still represents the current workplace.

For example, if a **healthcare emergency department** model takes months to create, then by the time the model reaches the analysis phase, the emergency department itself would have changed and the analytic results are useless.

The speed of model development is mostly determined by the tool and its requirements. Simulation tools that require more extensive programming takes longer to reach and complete the analysis phase. Especially, if the software requires the model analyzer to know the details of the programming environment.

Model animation represents the progress of the simulation. It does not have to be video-quality animation. It only needs to provide a visualization. This helps the model developers and audience understand the environmental constraints. In fact, pretty graphics can be a disadvantage in this stage. Displays can distract the team and audience from the main goal of the project.

For example, if an animation shows a nurse transporting a patient from a waiting room to pre-op, the details of how the nurse moves are not relevant to the analysis as long as the path is correct. The implementation may distract the group from concentrating on the travel distance if audience members are paying attention to the way the nurse's arms move in the animation.

To summarize: first, model development must be completed expediently without compromising its accurate representation of the flow, and second, the model itself must be designed so that it can be analyzed quickly without advanced programming knowledge.

MODEL OBSERVATION

At the start of the analysis phase, the development team needs to spend time observing the model animation and its resulting behavior. The team must understand the interdependent relationships:

- Between parts of the model and
- Be able to provide:
  - o detailed, easily-understandable explanations of the model behavior,
  - o boundary conditions, and
  - o causes and effects of bottlenecks.

These explanations must include information about:

- Flow constraints,
- Impact on the schedule,
- Equipment constraints, and
- Generated statistical data.

This observation also allows the team to identify behavior that should be modified. Sometimes, outdated procedures are still in place due to past conditions that have since been resolved. These steps may now be removed and cycle time improved with minimal changes to the operation. The team should ask why each step is required and examine the potential impact of eliminating any steps or procedures within the process flow.

Observation can also help the team to identify solutions to some of the detected bottlenecks. As the animation develops and entities flow through the model, the team can visualize the causes and conditions that lead to bottlenecks. Understanding these conditions can be a large advantage in the analysis results.

GOAL-BASED MODEL METRICS

Earlier, during the validation phase, a current state run should have been completed and compared to real-life data. This comparison involved a set of metrics that were used to map the model output to the live environment.

Like the validation phase, the analysis phase also requires a set of metrics to be defined in order to perform in-depth analysis and optimization. There are many different metrics that might be used. Generating too much data will lengthen and complicate the analysis phase and the team's understanding of the results. Not all metrics that were useful in the validation phase are useful in the analysis phase.

By identifying the key metrics to analyze in the model, analysis and optimization can be simplified and modeling efficiency increased. It is important to look back at the initial goal of the model and, if multiple types of analysis are required, prioritize them in order of importance.

One school of thought is to capture as much data as possible, then use external data analytics in order to determine the changes required. This strategy can generate an overwhelming amount of data and forces the modelers to spend more time analyzing the data than analyzing the model behavior itself.

This flawed method is normally used when the selected tool does not have a good visual representation of the simulation engine behavior. The animation should always represent what the simulation engine is doing and its state. Post-simulation animations and delayed animation effects do not serve this purpose.

Instead of compiling as many metrics as possible, let simulation goals drive the identification of the required metrics. List the simulation goals in order of importance. Then, for each goal, identify three key metrics that represent the performance of the goal.

For example, in a **capacity analysis model**, the three metrics are the number of entities completed, the rate of completion, and the ratio of VAT to total lead time (lean efficiency) of the objects. Those values can be computed regardless of industry: patients are the entities in healthcare, items picked are the entities in a warehouse, and items produced are the entities in manufacturing.

If the goal relates to a specific entity type (such as a particular patient acuity or manufacturing part), the team needs metrics representing the entity type in question *and* similar metrics regarding global model performance. The global model performance metrics are necessary because optimization of any specific entity type should not negatively impact the overall performance of the model. The added metrics are used to ensure that as capacity for a particular entity is increased, other entity types' capacities do not get affected.

One common goal is to reduce wait times, whether that relates to the patient waiting room, staging area, Kanban size or storage, and so on. Forcing wait times in the "waiting" processes and then artificially reducing those times may seem like a logical idea. In actuality it does not provide any useful information. All that the team can learn from such an action is that manipulating the wait time impacts the model in some way. An obvious conclusion that does not require a simulation. (For more on forced wait times, see Chapter 5: Data Collection.)

Instead, proper analysis of wait times should include:

- Metrics that show the size of the waiting or buffer area,
- Length of time an entity waits before proceeding to the next station, and
- Throughput of the flow at the station following the buffer process.

After identifying the goal-based metrics, there are other metrics for the team to add. Some should relate to the animation observation, covering specific areas that impact the simulation goal indirectly. These might include waiting for the next operation to complete (which normally identifies potential bottlenecks upstream from the process) or improper balancing of the flow.

Some necessary standard metrics also include process utilization at key process steps, process efficiencies, and resource utilization. All three of these metrics provide additional insight into model improvement as optimization occurs. They are covered later in this chapter.

In models with failure rates introduced on the processes, it is important to add metrics specific to these topics. Especially when identifying random failures throughout the operation. These metrics should measure the number of failures, the average, and maximum duration of the recovery at key process steps.

For these metrics to be useful, the process failures need to occur within a reasonable range that impacts the model during normal operation. Unusual, low-frequency failures, for example, should be considered exceptions that are handled as separate scenarios within the analysis process, *not* standard failures.

METRICS DATA CAPTURE, TIME INTERVALS, AND OTHER ADVICE ABOUT DATA

The frequency of metrics data capture is also an important consideration. If a model is running on a one-second time unit interval and events are occurring at 30 seconds, then capturing data on the second interval is meaningless. It produces too much data to be analyzed. Instead, capturing data at the minute interval reduces the amount of generated data to a more manageable quantity.

A normal practice is to start the data capture at intervals not exceeding the time of the fastest process to track in the model. In most cases, the interval may be even longer—up to 3 or 4 times the fastest process. It is up to the modeler to determine the interval sequence that provides the correct amount of data for the needs of the project.

Once a frequency is identified, it should be used for all future model analysis and iterations. This practice reduces potential data interpretation and scalability errors when comparing different scenarios. (The importance of choosing a consistent frequency is discussed at more length in Chapter 10: Detailed Analysis and Optimization.)

The duration of the simulation run also needs to be defined for all current and future state analysis. Every model runs through a warm-up phase where objects progress through the model until at least one "final" object is completed. A patient leaving an ED, a final assembly ready to store and ship, or a pick sequence that has passed through staging and is ready to be loaded onto a truck.

This warm-up phase allows the model internals to load up with parts so the model can reach a steady state. Some tools allow for initial state loading. This reduces the warm-up phase and allows the model to achieve a steady state more quickly. Other tools provide a way to reset the collected data to eliminate generated data bias created during the warm-up period.

The ability to reset the data collection during the simulation run is a hallmark of interactive simulation, which allows modification to the model as it runs in real-time. As changes to the model are applied during the run, the simulation includes multiple scenarios that cloud the results. Resetting the data collection corrects these results by eliminating the effect of multiple scenarios and allowing modelers to generate quick and accurate analysis of the current scenario.

The reset data collection environment is preferable due to its usefulness and speed of optimization. Loading the initial data set and preloading the model with entities is also a common practice if the simulation tool allows this to be done.

Differences in tools serve as a reminder to look at the basic model development and visualization capabilities of any simulation technology. Also to investigate its analysis options. Interactive analysis of the data and the ability to reset data collection are important for optimization and accurate analysis.

After reaching a steady state, the simulator should run for at least 3 times the duration of the timespan to be analyzed. For example, if the model is analyzing an ED where the patient arrival rate is based on a distribution curve and the treatment types and times are randomized, and if the goal is to analyze the ED for one month, then the simulation should run for at least 3 months. Depending on the model variability, Monte Carlo analysis may need to be performed for each potential solution.

If patient arrival is based on actual historical data, the model only needs to run the loaded data. Monte Carlo analysis may be required depending on the variability of the treatment cycle time characteristics.

As a general rule, if actual data is available and can represent a long enough time period, then the model run can be defined by the amount of data available. Provided it represents a large enough sample for analysis.

Loading the actual data set comes with another advantage: the modeler can quickly validate the results of the initial or current state. The outcome of this historical data is known, therefore the modeler has a clear idea of how close the model is to the real-world environment. Historical data provides 99%+ accuracy for the model in relation to the live environment.

When the actual data set is not available, for example in cases of new environments under analysis, data sets from similar environments can suffice. It may not be exactly representative. It does provide a good distribution and comparison for analysis purposes.

Data sets can also be modified and expanded. If historical data is used, it is possible to have the model run based on an increased required capacity, such as increasing patient arrivals by 10% or increasing the number of orders to pick by 15%. Some modeling environments allow for quick data manipulation in order to expand the loaded data and inject it with additional data points to simulate increased system requirements.

These tools also have the ability to create new data sets based on specific criteria that put the model through different scenarios without impacting the model logic. For example, a data creator environment can simulate an increased number of patients to an ED with orthopedic injuries in order to test seasonal changes by injury type.

In a **warehouse environment**, the data creator can represent an increased picking requirement for specific items, allowing the modeler to experiment with slotting or other picking strategies. In a **manufacturing environment**, the new data set can represent a new production schedule that imposes greater requirements out of the sub-components necessary to build the assemblies. These data creator system environments can provide a better representation of the live environments, especially in data-driven simulation models.

EFFICIENCY AND UTILIZATION IN ANALYSIS

After the generation of the initial or current state, the team needs to identify a number of scenarios to run and analyze. While observing the model and analyzing the data of the initial results, the team should have identified the potential bottlenecks or choke points in the system.

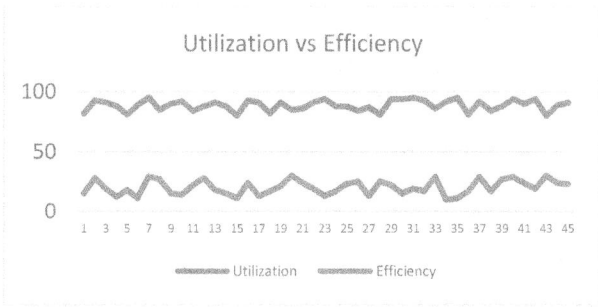

Image 9-1. Graph demonstrating utilization as compared to efficiency. This graph indicates a busy operation with excessive non-VAT.

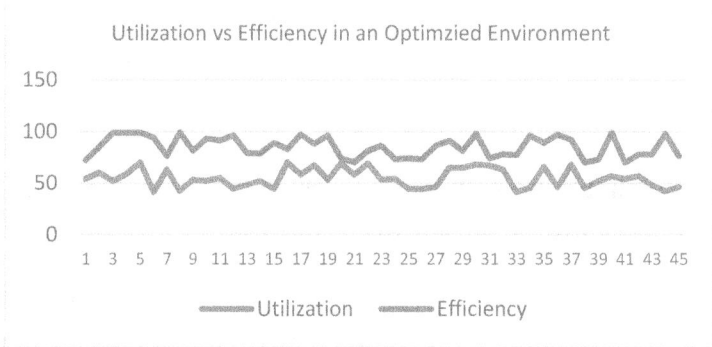

Image 9-2. Graph demonstrating utilization as compared to efficiency in an optimized environment. This graph represents a target: an efficient and busy environment. Here, the operation runs close to its designed throughput and close to its maximum capacity. This operation is highly efficient and has additional capacity available for future expansion.

As discussed in Chapter 2, efficiency refers to the ratio of VAT to lead time. It measures how well the process works and how much time is wasted. Utilization refers to what percentage of the resources are being used at a given time. Efficiency, therefore, should be as high as possible, but what about utilization? Should the goal be to use 100% of one's resources at all times?

Not necessarily. The actual utilization depends on many factors, including the MTBF, the MTTR, and any scheduled maintenance. There are times when the process cannot accept new entities; an operating room needs to be cleaned, a picking area needs replenishment, a fork truck goes down, etc.

(Once the distinction between a production item and a patient is reduced, a healthcare environment is actually very similar to a manufacturing environment; room cleaning is essentially process changeover.)

If MTBF/MTTR, changeover, and regular maintenance are entered into the system, the modeler's goal is to achieve 100% utilization because realistic limits to productivity have already been entered. The process efficiency does not actually hit 100%. The goal should be to increase efficiency as much as possible without affecting the quality of the process.

In the case where MTBF/MTTR, changeover, and regular maintenance are *not* entered, the process utilization step should be capped at a reasonable upper limit (80% for example), or the OEE of the process. Pushing the process beyond the designated upper limit under these circumstances generates results that are unachievable in a real-world environment.

Another key consideration is the object efficiency on the flow. This percentage is often a good indicator of how much improvement the overall process flow can achieve.

The object efficiency is computed as the sum of all the VAT in the flow as a percentage of the overall object lead time. For example, if an object (patient, pick sequence, part, etc.) takes two hours to go through the overall model, yet it only incurs 20 minutes of VAT, then the object flow is highly inefficient at a 16.6% efficiency rating.

The object efficiency should be computed at different intervals of the model, thereby providing a more targeted representation of where delays may occur and potential improvement may be achieved. Healthcare facilities are often more accustomed to such metrics because they frequently measure different segments of the patient visit (patient-to-physician time, disposition-to-discharge time, etc.).

A simulation environment that reports the object efficiency on the flow makes it easier to spot potential issues. Especially when multiple object types are being used (such as different levels of acuity, items to pick, or parts to produce). By analyzing the efficiency of each object, it is possible to spot the object that has the most delays and use the object flow to identify potential improvements.

RESOURCE ANALYSIS

In cases where manpower is entered into the model, resources usually represent a limiting constraint in relation to capacity and object efficiency. It is common to have resource delays due to shift allocation, lack of resource availability, or extended walk time between stations. There are many ways to analyze the resource impact on the model. As a rule, the following are a sequence of analysis steps that can help to identify whether resources are a constraint and to what level they impact the flow.

As an initial implementation of the resources, it is recommended to:

- Assume that they have no shifts (that is, they are always available),
- Have a high efficiency rating throughout the day, and
- Do not have to walk between stations if they are not carrying or moving with an entity.

In other words, the resource analysis should concentrate initially on a best case scenario for the resources.

Note that resources that are responsible for moving entities or objects should be implemented based on speed and distance factors in order to better analyze their impact. In many cases, resource movement is not entered at all or is averaged out to a specific duration that renders the model highly inaccurate.

Transitions between stations when moving entities or parts are critical in spotting potential resource constraints. Once the resources have been set up, the model run should identify the utilization of the resources and each process or transition wait time to acquire the resource.

If the utilization of one or more resources is high (more than 80%), a resource constraint exists and can worsen when all other factors are entered in. Alternatively, if the resource utilization is less than 80%, the modeling team needs to examine the time a process or transition waits to acquire the resource. If that number is larger than a single unit of simulation time, then a potential constraint also exists for that resource. Even though the utilization is low, or within acceptable range, resource sharing can have an impact on model capacity and efficiency.

Another important aspect to review when considering efficiency and utilization is the actual flow of entities and resources. A spaghetti diagram is useful for this purpose in order to 1) verify that the flow is correct, and 2) identify heavy traffic areas that cause congestion and potential future delays. Some simulation tools on the market today include the spaghetti diagram as part of their built-in analysis toolset.

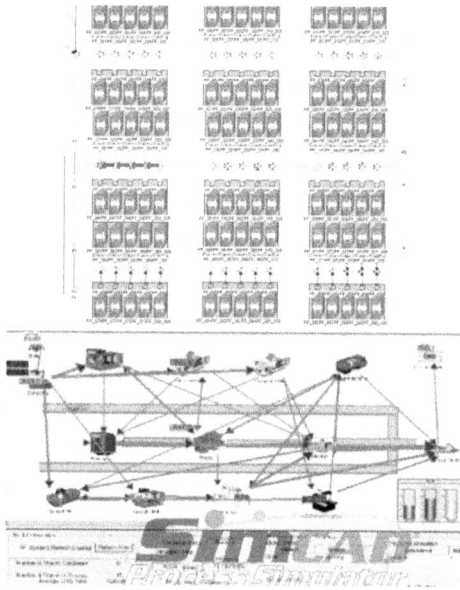

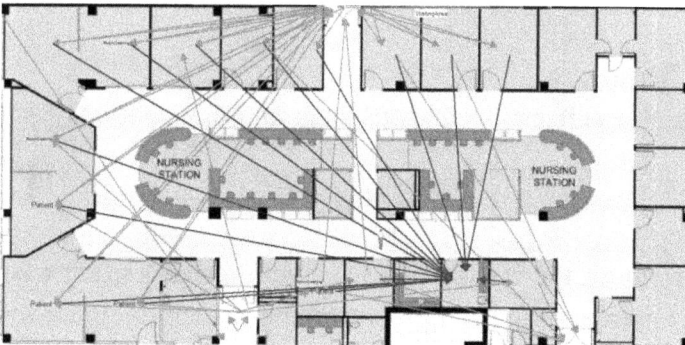

Sample spaghetti diagrams (based on path and direct connect) – Image 9-3

The spaghetti diagram was first introduced as part of lean analysis for high mix, low volume manufacturing operations. Its uses do not end there. It should be used extensively in all industries and configurations due to the enhanced analysis and visualization of trafficked areas it provides for both entities and resources alike.

Another useful diagram to review is the congestion analysis diagram. This diagram is similar to the spaghetti diagram but it represents the congestion factor of each section of the model. In contrast to the spaghetti diagram that displays the amount of traffic going through each section, only congested traffic is displayed in the congestion analysis diagram. Therefore the diagram indicates areas of the flow where congestion occurs so that it can be addressed and corrected.

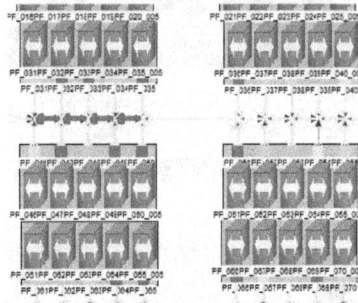

Sample congestion analysis diagram – Image 9-4

TRANSITIONS AND PATH IMPLEMENTATIONS

After performing the initial analysis on the resources, the next step of resource analysis is to examine transition behavior between stations when the resource does not carry or is not required for an entity.

Basically, the model at this point needs to request that the resource walk to its required location, perform a task or move an entity, then travel to the next destination to perform another task. This added behavior impacts both the resource utilization and the wait for the resource at the processes. If both of those attributes are unaffected, then the transition of resources when they are not carrying an entity has no impact on the model.

In most cases, an added waiting-for-resource time is observed (unless the resources are highly scheduled and the flow is a deterministic flow, in which case the simulation analysis does not need to expand the resources). Key parameters must also be observed such as:

- Percent of time traveling empty,
- Distance of travel while empty,
- Number of times a resource touches an entity, and
- Any in-shift fluctuation in demand for the resource.

Note that in order to get the most out of this type of analysis, the resource needs to travel correctly through aisles and pathways. Not through walls and equipment. Proper resource path implementation needs to exist.

Some simulation tools force the users to implement a separate connection or path for each potential path the resource takes. Then couple that with the object potential paths. These models become extremely cumbersome to use and update.

Other more advanced tools allow for path implementations that allow the modeler to simplify the model and reuse paths for objects. Moreover, these tools include optimizations such as shortest distance and fastest path options that the resource and objects can follow. This also has a great impact on the modeling environment and readability of the model.

IMPLEMENTING SHIFTS

The last step of resource analysis involves the implementation of shifts and resource availability. This step should only be performed after applying resources with and without travel as described above. The value of shifts stems from a few model constraints which are described below. Shifts should be implemented into the model if:

The resources utilize staggered shifts, where shifts overlap to avoid any flow delays and to allow some processes to start sooner than others in order to maintain a steady entity flow. An example would be starting a process an hour early in order to have enough work in progress so the line downstream does not starve. Normally, when staggered shifts are used, the number of available resources varies between shifts, which creates an added constraint on the model.

The operation runs continuously 24 hours a day, but the number of resources varies between shifts. This scenario is common in many industries, especially in healthcare. In a hospital setting, for example, some nurses' shifts span a few weeks instead of the more common one-week implementation. A nurse may work Tuesday and Thursday for one week, work the weekend the following week, and so on. The shift definition may also vary among nurses and other providers. The simulation tool must be able to quickly identify the shift constraint and allow the modeler to implement the proper availability of the resource for a variety of shift durations. This type of feature is not common in simulation software. It is only available in select modeling environments. Proper tool use is imperative in order to avoid extensive modeling detail requirements.

Breaks vary. Analyzing the effect of a 15 minute break and a 30 minute lunch break throughout the shift is important, as the lack of processing during these times reduces the overall capacity and sometimes creates line starvation. Staggered shifts can become a solution to line starvation.

Resource availability varies. If only capacity constraint is required, the shift may be replaced with a resource availability factor. For example, using 80% resource availability makes the resource available to the model for approximately 7.2 hours of productivity in a 9 hour shift. In many models, this scenario would serve as a good approximation of reality, especially when shifts are not staggered. The resource availability may also be used to support half a resource. Setting the resource availability to 50% would only allocate the resource based on the utilization and the model requirement.

In order to approximate an 80% normal workday availability for a person, half a resource would equate to 40% availability and not 50%. Mistakenly assuming 50% availability normally leads to increased capacity that cannot be achieved in the real-life process.

With the shifts defined, the modeler needs to assign the shifts to resources (and sometimes processes) in order to support the shift constraint. As with all other analysis implementations, the changes need to be validated before any meaningful analysis can be done.

The progress of this analysis is similar to the basic resource implementation. The only difference is that once shifts are defined, the resource utilization should be based on shift utilization, not daily utilization. Put another way, resource activity time is viewed based on the shift daily duration, 9 hours for example, and *not* based on a full 24-hour day.

If a resource's shift utilization is 80% (for example, working for 7.2 hours in a 9-hour shift), its daily utilization would be 30% (working for 7.2 hours in a 24-hour day). Analyzing the wrong value leads to incorrect assumptions about resource availability and utilization and generates errors in the final results of the simulation analysis.

If the operation runs 24/7 with breaks where the number of resources does not change between shifts, then the daily utilization computation method works correctly and shifts do not need to be implemented.

AUTOMATION, BINS, AND GUIDED VEHICLES

In the case of automation, the analysis sometimes requires a determination of how many reusable bins or guided vehicles should be used in order to better run the operation.

In the case of bins, the simulation should provide the minimum number required in order to avoid inefficiencies due to the unavailability of the bins. Some more advanced tools have built-in methods to allow the model to compute the minimum number of bins required in order to achieve the desired behavior.

The key to promoting accuracy in this analysis is that the model must have failure and rework built in, properly implemented, and validated. Computing the number of bins required without the failure rates generates incorrect results and should be avoided. Furthermore, any line delays or wait due to system activities should be implemented with 0 timing in order to avoid additional cycle times in the model.

The same strategy can serve to identify the number of guided vehicles required to run the operation. However, guided vehicle analysis requires more detail on attributes such as the path, duration to load/unload, battery charge method, and discharge rate of the batteries. As with bin analysis, failure rates on the different equipment need to be implemented in addition to the constraints of the vehicle itself.

Analysis of guided vehicles, and material handling analysis in general, is a common task requested of simulation models. Due to the cost of the equipment, the congestion it imposes, safety as it relates to people crossing, and impact on the overall throughput, material handling analysis is at the core of every operation and should be performed thoughtfully and carefully.

Similar to the analysis of resources, the analysis of material handling equipment follows a specific set of iterations that simplify the task of finding the optimal amount of equipment and examining the performance of the system. Unfortunately, most material handling simulations concentrate on the visual appeal of the model rather than the actual model behavior and its relationship to the real-life systems.

When analyzing guided vehicle and material handling systems, the following are some key metrics to monitor and collect for use in the optimization cycle:

Identify the "useful utilization" of each vehicle that is active at any point during the simulation run. This utilization is computed based on the amount of time the vehicle is carrying an item for delivery, and should not include charge time, maintenance time, or traveling empty to pick up. This is the key metric that identifies the actual time the vehicle is busy performing an activity.

Identify the time that each vehicle is idle and waiting for a mission. After the downtime, maintenance, charging, and empty travel is implemented in the model, this metric provides a view into any potential extra capacity available per vehicle. It is important to measure these metrics on a vehicle-by-vehicle basis in order to optimize the number of vehicles required and clean up their schedules.

Identify the time the vehicle is available before someone needs to charge it, replace its batteries, or perform regular maintenance. These values are especially important if the actual mission travel distance varies due to the spatial dimensions of the facility or the weight of the item carried; these cases make it harder to predict battery discharge, so analysis from the model can be particularly useful. If charging analysis needs to be performed, the vehicles' discharge rates must be implemented within the model and actual recharge time must be requested when the charge level is within a set limit. In an optimized environment, achieving proper charging cycles can lead to a more efficient utilization of the fleet and an improvement in overall system performance.

Identify metrics from the requesting processes. If a vehicle needs to pick up an entity from one location and deliver it to another, the amount of time the entity waits before it is picked up becomes a critical element in identifying the buffer sizes at each process pick up and drop off point.

The time a vehicle waits at a destination to unload and deliver the entity. High values here normally indicate that the process is too slow to accept the delivered entity within the required constraints. This issue can be caused by a capacity constraint on the process or a simple scheduling problem that is creating a bottleneck at the process.

Warehousing, distribution centers, and supply chain type models also need to have metrics identifying storage density. For example, if items are stored on a rack, what percentage of the rack volume is empty? In detailed models and when rack density is low, it becomes more important to identify the density by location in order to better understand the storage requirement.

For all of the above metrics, it is critical to analyze the values over time. Do not rely only on averages and min/max parameters! The averages often mask the true cause of the problem, while min/max parameters provide boundary conditions for space and time constraints. The true analysis of the model is to view the variability through time for each parameter and compare the graphs in order to determine the actual problem to be solved.

RECAP

This chapter addresses some of the simpler strategies available for analyzing the model data to understand the real-life operation in more depth. The analysis phase is the time to reap the fruits of the labor completed in the earlier phases.

Beyond the introductory considerations of this chapter, the analysis phase has even more to offer. The following chapter addresses more detailed analysis and optimization methods.

Chapter 10: Analyzing the Flow and Optimization

The analysis phase contains three steps.

1. Identifying and collecting metrics.
2. Analyzing the flow and the collected metrics,
3. Optimizing the simulation in order to generate a more efficient solution to the problems.

This chapter focuses on steps two and three.

The previous chapter discussed the first step mentioned above: the metrics necessary for analysis and the fact that averages are often unreliable for analysis and optimization. Analyzing the metrics through time and observing the model behavior through animation are both more effective methods of identifying bottlenecks and optimizing the flow.

Model observation is very important in the overall process and must not be overlooked regardless of model complexity. If a picture is worth a thousand words, then a simulation is worth a thousand pictures.

Many modelers discount the usefulness of simulation observation. These misguided modelers end up wasting time examining endless sets of generated metrics rather than quickly identifying the problem through the animation and connecting back into the data.

Having accurate animation in relation to the simulation engine is the key to making the most of simulation observation. A post-animation representation of the model is only useful for visualization and presentation. A real-time representation of the simulation engine progress with animation helps in both visualization and analysis. This feature should be investigated prior to investing in a simulation tool.

Another feature that comes in handy in the optimization phase is the ability to make changes during the simulation run. The ability to visually understand the cause and effect of each change and see the system reaction when a constraint is modified helps in understanding the process relationships and the effect of each constraint on the system.

As discussed in Chapter 8: Model Validation, tools that do not provide real-time model changes require the modeler to make the change, validate the change, start the simulation, wait for the steady state to be reached, observe the simulation, and repeat the cycle for each constraint to be modified.

On the other hand, tools with real time-modification ability during the run allow the team to start the simulation, wait for steady state, make and validate the change while the model is running, observe, make another change, etc. The time required to perform the same task without the dynamic interaction can easily be 5 to 10 times longer than in environments where real-time updates are possible.

Understanding the cause and effect of the constraints is considered the main driver of the analysis phase. Depending on the tool being used, the analysis phase may be extensive and requires multiple simulation runs.

Regardless of the type of tool being used, the analysis phase requires the modeler to collect data through time for the key metrics of the model. Each of the collected data sets should be based on the same frequency in order to properly map the time factor into the simulation results.

The confusion that can arise from different data collection frequencies is illustrated below.

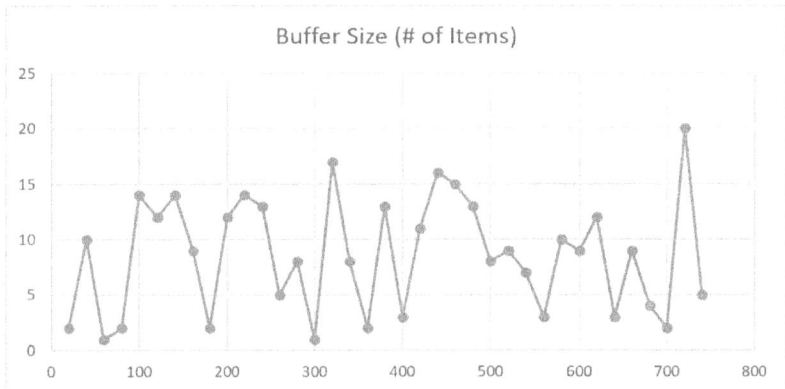

Image 10-1. Buffer data recorded on 20 minute interval.

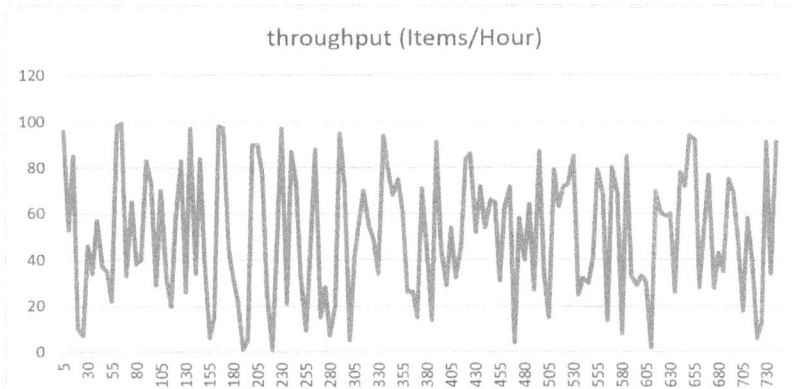

Image 10-2. Throughput recorded on a 5 minute interval.

The graphs above (Images 10-1 and 10-2) represent two data sets based on two different data collection frequencies. The graph with the larger frequency (20 minute interval) hides more data than the graph with smaller frequency. Visually comparing the graphs is difficult because each graph's scale is different. Therefore, in order to simplify the analysis phase and properly convey the results to the model customers, it is critical that the same data collection frequency be used throughout.

The collected data for multiple runs and scenario may be quite extensive. If the modeler can quickly modify the model and make a new run, more data sets are available for the analysis phase. This capability allows for more efficient analysis and less time spent poring over an overwhelming data set.

Comparing the different scenarios and the results within a simulation run is a requirement for every simulation project. If the tool being used does not provide a comparison capability, the modeling team needs an external tool that allows them to export data and perform offline analysis. Microsoft Excel® is a common tool for this purpose due to its ability to graph and compare large data sets.

It is recommended to use a tool that includes a built-in data analysis section with export capability. Having the scenario analyzer built into the simulation environment eliminates the need for an additional data management environment and allows for faster data analysis and model comparisons.

EXAMINING THROUGHPUT GRAPHS

With multiple model runs completed and proper metrics collected, the modeler needs to review and compare the generated results. This can be done by comparing similar metrics from different runs and analyzing the constraint effect on the model. While such a procedure sounds simple, the analysis can become complicated and convoluted.

To simplify the task and pinpoint the causes of any problems, start by identifying the key graphs that represent the output that relates most closely to the goal.

In the case of **capacity analysis**, identify the system throughput, number of active entities, and lead time. In the case of **resource utilization analysis**, identify data regarding resource utilization, time spent waiting for the resource, and resource travel. In the case of **material handling equipment**, identify the percent of time the vehicle has an item, its maintenance schedule, and the empty travel time. It is important to look at the analysis through time and not as an average or min/max, as discussed in Chapter 9: Basic Analysis.

The graphs can represent several different states:

- The model ramps up one or more of the values and enters a steady state with little or no variation of the values.
- The model ramps with one or more values constantly changing throughout the run. The graph(s) would then contain a number of spikes and valleys depending on the model variability.
- The model values ramp up, hits a steady state, and then enter another set of variability. The cycle repeats. This option is a combination of the previous two states.

The following images are graphs representing these states, followed by more detailed discussions.

RAMP UP TO STEADY STATE

In this case, the model ramps up one or more of the values and enters a steady state with little or no variation of the values.

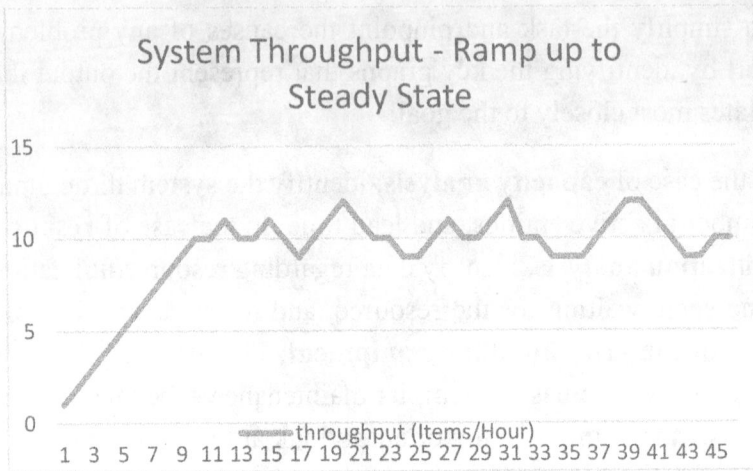

Image 10-3. System throughput per hour as the system ramps up to steady state.

This scenario (Image 10-3) indicates that one or more constraints are limiting the production. Or the system is close to its capacity limits. The only way to find out is to examine additional metrics that indicate high utilization and low efficiency, which in turn means a constraint is causing excessive wait time.

Start from the end of the flow and work back to the start to identify the first set of highly inefficient processes or transfers. In general, the first process identified is the flow constraint and its limits should be addressed.

Note that the limit to increase is not, and should never be, the buffer. All that a buffer increase does is delay the bottleneck; it still occurs at a later time. That issue can be referred to as "hurry up and wait" syndrome, in which the flow is pushed as fast as possible to a constraining process that is limiting the overall operation.

If the entities cannot be processed toward the end of the flow or where the process constraint is, there are two options. Either more capacity needs to be added at the location of the constraint, or previous operations need to be slowed down.

Unfortunately, "hurry up and wait" syndrome is a common problem across industries. It stems from scheduling inefficiencies and a lack of downstream visibility. A common symptom of such a system is high WIP in the flow.

For example, consider a clinic that always has a full waiting room. Although the goal of the clinic is to see as many patients as possible in a day, scheduling more patients than the clinic capacity during regular hours creates a backup.

High WIP operations in manufacturing and busy staging areas in warehouses face a similar problem. A warehouse may be very efficient in picking and getting orders ready in the staging area, but if trucks are not available on time to load the orders, then the staging area becomes congested. The picking team is performing as efficiently as possible, but orders must wait due to a constraint downstream.

Lean manufacturing concepts such as Kanban and pull systems specifically target this type of high WIP behavior. The problem is that most organizations have not made the connection between their flow and the actual constraint of the systems. Simulation is useful here. It can help identify the causes of any potential bottlenecks. Plus provide feedback on scheduling limitations and other solutions to the problem.

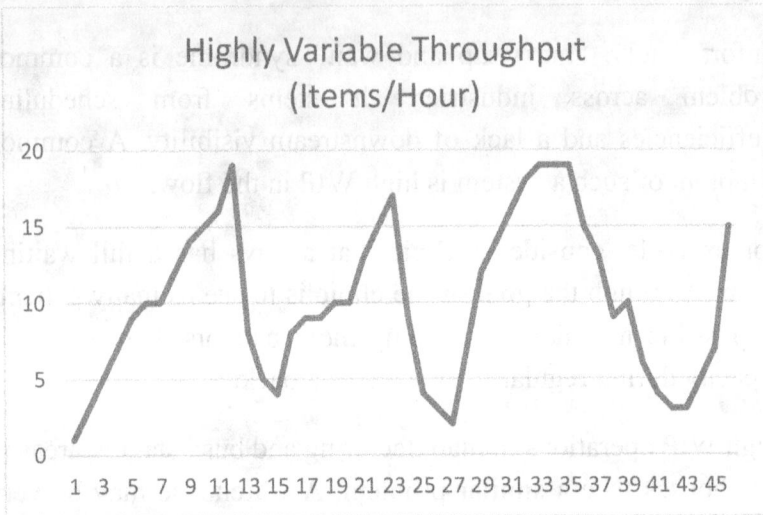

Image 10-4. An example of highly variable throughput per hour.

Image 10-4 indicates a highly variable line. The throughput is constantly changing, which causes problems downstream. Sometimes, in an attempt to control the variability, a supermarket concept is implemented, but this addition often results in high WIP.

WIP is expensive to produce, store and maintain. It directly affects the overall cash flow of the operation. WIP decreased is money saved; any reduction to WIP increases a project's ROI.

This type of graph is the result of an improperly load leveled line with incorrect buffering. The process steps within the model may have a large variation in their cycle time properties, break down too often, have a high change over time, or be buffered incorrectly.

To properly analyze these systems, the modeler needs to generate data that relates to the buffer capacities throughout the flow and correlate the throughput of the system with buffer capacities and loads.

To determine the cause of the spikes (that is, the cause of the problem), the modeler must generate graphs for metrics that precede the graph spike.

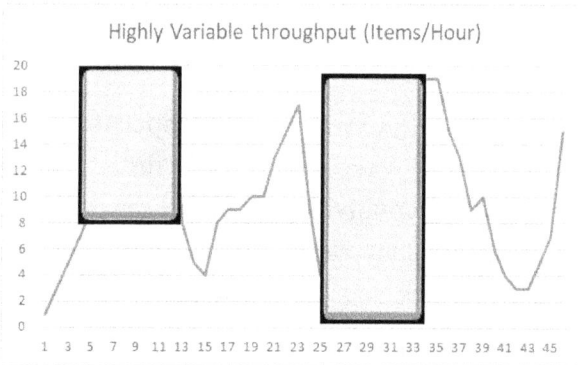

Image 10-5. Highlighted areas indicate the time span that should be reviewed in order to determine the cause of the spike.

By examining the changes in the model that resulted in the spike, the modeler is able to determine the metrics that lead to the increased level of throughput.

The same concept applies to determining the cause of the dip in throughput. Note that in many cases, the cause for throughput delay is caused by downstream processes. It is therefore important to analyze metrics from both upstream and downstream process steps in order to find the cause of the fluctuation.

Another cause of the unbalanced line may be the schedule that is driving the operation. Examining this schedule of orders and entities requested from the flow can unearth the true cause of the issue.

To test this theory, the modeler needs to switch the model schedule to either an evenly distributed flow or a more even distribution of processing from the line. For example, if the production line for a manufacturing operation is driven by a schedule of items to produce, the modeler needs to eliminate the time to induct the order into the model and switch the model to pull from the schedule for the next order as the production environment capacity allows.

The same advice applies to **warehousing operations**. The spikes may be related to the wave picking and distribution of orders through the wave. Alternatively, the wave generation itself may be generating the unbalanced environment due to inaccurate data that is feeding the pick sequence generation. Another cause in warehousing may be the slotting system not taking into consideration elements such as congestion and strike zone slotting for picked items. These elements, in turn, generate a variable throughput environment.

In a **healthcare implementation** of a surgical center, the spike is most likely related to incorrect scheduling or lack of providers' ability to be on time for the surgery. Another common issue is the misalignment of the schedule to the actual time required to perform the surgeries and their relationships to the cleaning and surgical carts pull.

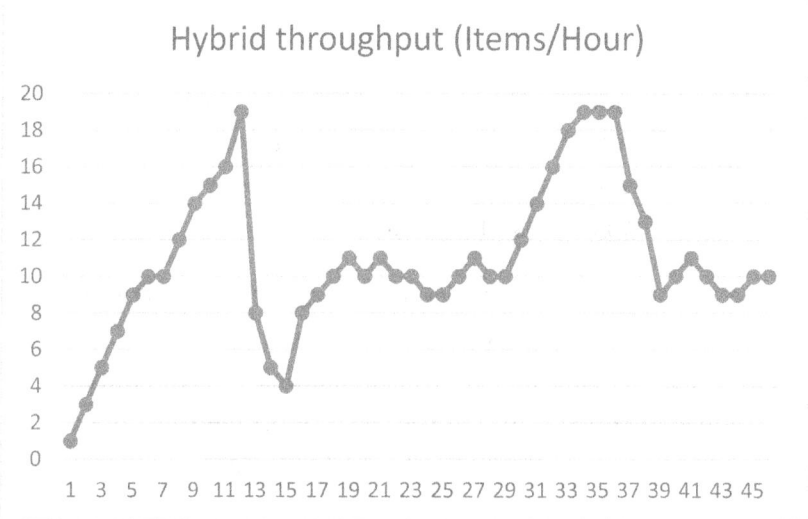

Image 10-6. An example of hybrid throughput over time.

The third scenario (Image 10-6) is a hybrid of the first and second scenarios. As such, it can be addressed in a similar way to the second scenario (highly variable throughput) with a transition to the first (ramping up to steady state). The goal is to identify the cause of the spike in order to level the line, then determine ways to increase throughput as was done in the first scenario.

Regardless of the type of analysis required, or the type of metric being investigated, the same set of methods can be used as long as the modeler determines and identifies the relationships among the metrics collected. Using the wrong metrics to analyze the flow results in incorrect or incomplete analysis of the model.

OPTIMIZATION

Once the team has finished analyzing the model, team members must determine better ways to run the current operation. They must devise new guidelines in order to increase the overall efficiency. Optimization tools may be useful in determining new constraints to increase throughput or utilization, but these results may not always be feasible within the flow.

For example, in a **healthcare emergency department**, the optimization tool might suggest increasing the number of nurses from 5 to 10, adding two triage stations, and employing an additional ED doctor, all in order to support the flow and reduce patient wait time from 25 minutes to 3 minutes.

Although that may be a valid optimization, it is not economically feasible for the hospital to add the required staff. In addition, the modeler needs to explain the reasoning behind the increase in staff requirement when making a pitch for this change. Showing the model and comparing present and future states to demonstrate the improvement is one option, but the optimization tool only reveals the solution, not the root cause of the problem.

Presenting a solution without valid reasoning for the increased cost decreases the confidence level of the customers and audience in the simulation's capabilities. Therefore, optimization is best performed in a more detailed manner in order to come up with attainable solutions that address the root of the problem and achieve the desired results. A simulation optimization environment that generates unrealistic solutions is nothing but a valueless gaming exercise.

In order to optimize the flow, the modeler needs to understand the current system, the relationships between the processes, the scheduling implications, and the physical system limitations. As detailed in previous sections, performing a simulation for the sake of animation is much less involved and does not require the same level of data detail or understanding of the flow.

Proper analysis must include full understanding of the overall flow and constraints. This understanding, in many cases, can be achieved by observing the simulation animation over time and understanding the constraint relationships through generated time-based metrics.

When optimization starts, model changes are required in order to implement the behavior or constraint change. With every change performed, the model needs to be re-validated in order to make sure its integrity is not compromised and it still represents the actual system. This continuous validation is a key component of optimization that is often ignored for the sake of saving time, but it ends up generating incorrect results and recommendations.

TYPES OF OPTIMIZATION

There are many types of optimization. Different types of optimization require different knowledge and strategies in order to reach their full potential. This section discusses a few common optimization methods and provides advice about each one.

Interactive optimization. Modelers perform interactive changes to determine which one provides the optimum results. There are a couple of items to keep in mind when performing this type of optimization.

The modeler needs to be aware of any schedule variability into the model and potential spikes in requests due to the schedule sequence. All industries have similar constraints on the schedule, which can cause the modeler to lose track of the optimization goal. In cases where the schedule changes extensively, the model should be run based on a worst case run scenario while performing the interactive optimization.

The modeler needs to be able to reset the analysis data in order to perform the validation of the change and capture a correct set of metrics. Since resetting the analysis metrics eliminates the need to constantly restart the model, optimization can be performed at a much faster pace.

To perform interactive optimization and validation, the modeling team needs to interact with the model much like they might an interactive computer game. The modeler needs to apply small changes to the model, validate that the behavior has been applied, and study the effect of the change through the generated animation and model statistics.

The key here is that the tool should allow the modeler to make the change on the model during the simulation run, and implement the change on the model itself in order to impact the model flow. As better solutions are found, the modeler is able to reset the data collection in order to clear out the multiple data states generated by the change, then start analyzing the new data set that corresponds to the current model state.

Interactive optimization also helps in identifying system boundary conditions and analyzing specific scenarios in the model. For example, if a process (bed, machine, room, rack, staging, etc.) is unavailable for a period of time for extensive repair, the modeler should be able to temporarily suspend that process and study the effect on the simulation. Then, after the full delay is accomplished, the modeler can resume the suspended process in order to figure out a way to get the system back to its steady state.

Specific scenarios are generated out of this type of analysis identifying boundary conditions. For example, a scenario may identify that when a buffer is 70% full, then the system does not recover unless some upstream processes are suspended for a specific time duration.

The problem cannot be fixed by simply increasing the buffer. Because, the buffer is not the contributing factor to the problem. Instead, the solution should be to allow the downstream processes to temporarily increase capacity and prevent the buffer from reaching the limit. Although it is not always feasible to increase capacity, the scheduling system driving the operation needs to be aware of that condition and should adjust its sequencing in order to avoid the resulting behavior. These situations require a schedule optimization, not line modification. A new simulation goal should therefore be added to the project to include schedule optimization and to define scheduling guidelines.

If interactive optimization is used, the modeler needs to expand on manual optimization using scenarios. The team should perform multiple runs and generate analysis data for each scenario. The generated data sets need to be analyzed and compared in order to identify the potential optimization needed to achieve the desired results. This type of optimization relies on the ability of the modeling team to 1) identify the key processes or constraints that lead to inefficiencies, and 2) devise new methods in order to improve the flow.

If the simulation tool has an optimizer component, or if an optimization software is available, other attributes may need to be collected, maintained and passed to the optimization environment. This technology can be highly valuable to the team's optimization efforts, but it must be understood and used properly.

OPTIMIZATION ENGINE

When using an optimization engine, the modeler needs to be aware of its capabilities and connectivity to the simulation environment. There are two types of optimization systems: integrated and non-integrated.

In an **integrated system**, the optimization engine and the simulation tool are designed to work seamlessly together so that data from the simulation environment flows through to the optimization engine.

In a **non-integrated system**, the simulation model needs to create a data set that can be imported into the optimization engine. The optimization engine in this case is independent of the simulation environment.

Both implementations have their advantages and disadvantages, but in general an integrated optimizer provides a more consistent optimization method and results. There are many reasons for this consistency.

For one, in a non-integrated environment, the data set export/import process may be compromised and the data set misplaced. Another reason is the constraint transition between the simulation environment and the optimization engine; if one constraint is not properly transitioned and updated, the solution is invalid.

One more aspect to keep in mind is that in a non-integrated environment, the modeler is responsible for maintaining two separate systems that have to be constantly aligned, which increases model development time.

Some optimization environments have the ability to learn from the simulation environment. As different simulation scenarios are run, the simulation results are channeled to the optimizer data input stream along with any constraints that were imposed during the run (such as equipment failures, availability, and other factors). The optimizer is constantly running in the background and learning the behavior of the model and the relationship among all the generated data points.

Such optimizers are built on learning algorithms based on neural networks and genetic algorithms, which configure their internal structures based on the model behavior and the goals set for the optimization analysis.

After the optimizer completes its learning cycle, it is able to quickly answer questions about the system settings required to achieve a specific throughput or capacity goal. The optimizer results can then be applied to the model and a new analysis data run can be completed in order to validate the optimization results.

Learning optimizers are extremely useful when configured and used properly. Identifying which set of parameters the team should feed the learning engine sets the team up to achieve good optimization results. The more data point types the optimizer receives, the more scenarios it must run and provide data for.

Although the optimizer starts to ignore some of the metrics due to their lack of contribution to the model improvement, providing too much data to be analyzed slows down model runtime. For a learning optimizer to be effective, it has to be tightly integrated with the simulation environment in order to maximize runtime speed and the efficiency of the simulation project.

RECAP

While there are many methods of performing detailed analysis and optimization, this chapter has given an overview of several common strategies. Advice for examining throughput graphs and determining their meaning can take the team a long way in the analysis and optimization process, and learning how to avoid common pitfalls when optimizing can make the process more fruitful and efficient.

Having the ability to visually optimize using real-time model changes during the simulation run is by far the best method to improve the flow and learn the interdependency among processes and constraints.

Regardless of which optimization and analysis strategies are used, every solution needs to be validated using different schedules, the best case scenario, the average case, and all other possible scenarios that the system might encounter. All scenario-run metrics should be saved in a time-based analytics system that enables comparison through time for the collected scenarios.

It is important to note that in a highly variable environment, a set of Monte Carlo runs need to be performed on the optimized model to make sure that the newly implemented changes have a positive impact on the flow in all situations.

At this point, the entire simulation-building process has been discussed, from goal-setting to analysis and optimization. The following chapter addresses the influence that a simulation can have on one particularly tricky field: scheduling.

Success with Simulation

Chapter 11: Scheduling

Scheduling is a complicated endeavor for any business. Not only employees, but also tools, machinery, and spaces must all be coordinated. Resources must be used efficiently, and they also must be synchronized with each other so that, for example, a doctor has the space, staff, and tools she needs to operate on a patient. Every element must work together, but gaps while a person waits for a resource must be minimized.

New methods of scheduling can face resistance in a work environment, particularly from those who are accustomed to a longstanding tradition of doing things in a particular way. Those who suggest alternatives may be told that their ideas are unnecessary and that the scheduling patterns are fine the way they are.

It is important to remember that every business can become more efficient. The fact that one way "works just fine" does not mean that a new or different way does not work even better. Innovation, especially when based on a solid foundation of data, is important to every operation's growth and success.

By this point, it is clear that simulation has tremendous benefits to process optimization. But simulation can also serve other purposes, including a comprehensive examination of the operation as a whole, which aids an organization significantly in determining how to schedule its employees and other resources.

This chapter examines the benefits of simulation for scheduling purposes. This examination first focuses on commonplace scheduling methods used today, then transition to a set of ideas to help in devising an alternative scheduling strategy that uses historical data and evidence to cut down on wasted time.

A CLOSER LOOK AT COMMON SCHEDULING STRATEGIES

The scheduling methods used in business today can vary tremendously by industry and even by corporation. Any discussion of "today's scheduling strategies" inevitably generalize the practices of many organizations and cannot possibly incorporate the full variation found in the world of business practices.

Still, there are a few strategies that have gained attention and warrant a brief discussion. What are some of the scheduling methods that some companies use?

First of all, it is concerning to note that many scheduling managers do not use any scheduling technology at all when organizing their staff. In a 2016 survey of nurse managers, for example, 23% claimed not to use any kind of scheduling tool, 24% used paper-based tools, and 19% used digital spreadsheets.[37]

In a field like nursing, in which many hospitals are understaffed and fatigue can lead to low morale and medical errors, these statistics are cause for concern. Nurse managers are already overworked. Scheduling is only one of the tasks they must complete for their teams to run smoothly.

---

[37] "Nurse scheduling, staffing issues continue to afflict hospitals: 8 key statistics," *Beckers Hospital Review*, October 14, 2016, https://www.beckershospitalreview.com/human-capital-and-risk/nurse-scheduling-staffing-issues-continue-to-afflict-hospitals-8-key-statistics.html.

The use of some type of automated technology to alleviate this burden would go a long way toward improving working conditions for many nurses as well as helping hospitals to accomplish more with the resources they already have.

There are many organizations that do use scheduling tools and techniques. One strategy that has gained attention comes from the Aurora Medical Group, which has implemented a "scheduling wheel" to attempt to make the daily flow of appointments more standardized and predictable. This technique breaks every hour down into smaller pieces and fills them with different types of appointments—new patients, patients with acute conditions, administrative sessions for paperwork and phone calls, etc. At the top of every hour, the wheel repeats in the same order.[38]

This strategy aims to control variability in the workplace by creating consistent patterns and accounting for appointments that might take longer by using the administrative time at the end of the hour as a buffer.

A similar "wheel" format has been used in manufacturing as well. In this case, production for replenishment was organized to minimize changeover time on the machines.[39] Once again, the aim was to make complex patterns of demand more predictable.

---

[38] Tiffany Chan, "How Aurora Medical Group reinvented the scheduling wheel," *Advisory Board,* 1 October 2014. https://www.advisory.com/research/medical-group-strategy-council/practice-notes/2014/september/aurora-scheduling-wheel.

[39] Jaci Souza, Alan H. Nall, and Peter L. King, "Reinventing the production scheduling wheel," *APICS Magazine,* September/October 2017. http://www.apics.org/apics-for-individuals/apics-magazine-home/magazine-detail-page/2017/09/06/reinventing-the-production-scheduling-wheel.

What these strategies fail to take into account is that most workplaces have more variability than what can be controlled in a standardized "wheel" format. Rather than attempting to force the variations of a workplace to conform to a preconceived organizational pattern, simulation modeling can account for changing conditions and optimize the schedule to fit them.

Rather than choosing a schedule and sticking with it indefinitely, a business must be capable of scheduling and *rescheduling* when unpredictable events inevitably occur. This type of scheduling strategy involves taking historical data into account and predicting future trends. That is, doing exactly what simulation models do best.

Some advice does include the use of historical data. Physicians Practice, a website of information for medical professionals, suggests using data to identify trends and to establish a baseline for what the organization should consider "on-schedule." Then, the basic schedule should be adjusted to resolve any problems that occur.[40]

While this strategy might seem sound, it involves consistently playing catch-up to any conflicts or issues that may arise. A simulation, in contrast, would predict these issues before they occur and alert the scheduling staff in advance. This software would enable the company to be proactive, not reactive, in addressing potential problems.

One common scheduling trick in a **hospital setting** is to have less experienced residents perform the simpler surgeries and

---

[40] Judy Capko, "To Improve Practice Work Flow, Tackle Patient Scheduling," *Physicians Practice,* 27 May 2015, http://www.physicianspractice.com/scheduling/improve-practice-work-flow-tackle-patient-scheduling.

therefore free up more experienced residents and physicians to operate on more complicated cases. However, this strategy is a double-edged sword; while it does assign work based on skill, it can be very challenging to predict the amount of time a surgery takes when a less experienced resident is in charge.[41]

Simpler surgeries take longer when inexperienced staff are the ones operating. The operating room is occupied for a longer period of time to accomplish the same task. The scheduler must take into account the additional time required to perform the surgery in order for the surgery department supply chain and provider to be synchronized. Failure to do so results in increased inefficiencies and have a negative impact on the upstream and downstream processes.

Attempting to make an unpredictable workplace setting into a predictable one is not the most effective scheduling strategy. Rather than fearing and attempting to restrain this unpredictability, managers can embrace it and use simulation software to develop a scheduling plan that works for the company.

---

[41] Raul Pulido, Adrian M. Aguirre, Miguel Ortega-Mier, Alvaro Garcia-Sanchez, and Carlos A. Mendez, "Managing daily surgery schedules in a teaching hospital: a mixed-integer optimization approach," *BMC Health Services Research* 14 (2014): 472, https://doi.org/10.1186/1472-6963-14-464.

TRADITIONAL SCHEDULING

All of the above examples illustrate important details about the scheduling process. To paint with a broader brush, traditional scheduling is usually fairly similar across industries.

Each organization has one scheduler (or a scheduling team) who schedules the operation using knowledge acquired through years of experience. The scheduler knows the limits of the equipment, understands the products or processes to be completed, and has a global view of the operation.

Conventional wisdom would say that "the scheduler always knows" how best to allocate staffing and technological resources to meet demand. But is that true? And even if it is, what is the impact on the organization if the scheduler decides to move on to another position at a different company? Unfortunately, this is a common issue in both large and small organizations; there is no guarantee that the scheduler is around forever.

Relying on a scheduler with years of experience is one common but misguided strategy. Another frequent misconception in scheduling is to force constraints on the system based on information from many years ago. This situation happens most often in more mature organizations that have evolved through time.

When equipment and processes are modified, the scheduling limits are, more often than not, left intact. They continue to include constraints based on the old environment or process implementations that used to be valid but are no longer relevant.

Therefore, before going into modifying the current scheduling system and methods, one must question the validity of the imposed constraints. Do they still apply in the current environment? Each constraint that can be removed or simplified should be identified and validated in order to avoid potential inaccuracies in scheduling in the future.

A third common error in conventional scheduling has to do with the delivery or "ready by" date. Traditionally, scheduling implementations impose date and time delivery-by dates to all schedules, then enforce that constraint on the existing environment.

This technique actually operates in the wrong order. Rather than setting a deadline first and then arranging the schedule to meet it, the team should ask, "How do I schedule the work to be performed so that the operation is the most efficient?" Once the operation's efficiency is optimized, *then* the team should define specific scheduling deadlines.

This is a controversial point. Many people would say that scheduling should be organized around the time the customer needs the product or service performed. When the process has reached its maximum efficiency, its cost to the organization is substantially lower than it would be in a less efficient setup. The organization can then evaluate its operational savings and, if possible, decrease costs to the customer.

From a customer perspective, the product or service is completed on time, all the time, if the operation focuses first on efficiency and then on scheduling to maintain that efficiency. Needless to say, simulation can be used to justify the change, identify the proper guidelines, and determine the cost savings to the organization.

THE BENEFITS OF SIMULATION IN SCHEDULING

Every industry faces scheduling difficulties that can be mitigated or eliminated by first creating a simulation model of the process to understand and optimize it, then building a schedule to support this optimized version of the operation. Different industries face different challenges, but they can all benefit from incorporating simulation into their scheduling process.

For example, **healthcare** professionals struggle with extreme scheduling issues due to the inherent variability in the patient population and external conditions, while **warehousing** and distribution centers suffer from improper internal scheduling as it relates to external deliveries and internal system capabilities. **Manufacturing** and production systems face challenges of delayed production, excessive work in progress, and order variability.

One must ask: if scheduling systems are truly working the way they should, why do emergency departments require such large waiting rooms? Why do distribution centers have staging areas constantly overflowing with orders to ship? If traditional scheduling were sufficient to suit the needs of these organizations, such problems would not occur as frequently as they do.

A large share of scheduling errors come from using the wrong parameters, an incorrect goal, or incomplete information about the operation. Simulation modeling can address these sources of error and amend them.

For example, consider a **healthcare clinic** that constantly has a full waiting room. The scheduling is done based on standard ten-minute slices with a physician with the hope that eventually the schedule lines up. Appointments are organized without any reference to the patient condition. All it takes is a few appointments that exceed the ten-minute window for the whole day to end up behind schedule.

Instead of forcing the variability to fit into a pattern that it inevitably breaks, scheduling needs to be performed around the system variability. It needs to incorporate full knowledge of the operating environment, true understanding of the constraints, and feedback from the real-time systems on the progress and status of the operation.

Simulation helps the team to understand more fully the details of the operation and the impact of constraints on the system. Simply by running the model, the modeler can identify how the constraints affect the flow, where bottlenecks develop, and how to resolve them. There is tremendous value in watching the model and following the entities through the operation.

Meanwhile, the input data into the simulation environment sheds light on the different system capabilities and how each entity impacts its process. In addition, system limits are identified and detailed as part of the simulation modeling exercise. All of this information is valuable when the time comes to determine a schedule.

Keep in mind that the model runs at a much faster speed than the normal operation; it takes only minutes to view days of model progress. It is said that a picture is worth a thousand words, but an animated simulation is worth thousands of pictures. The main goal of watching the run is to learn the behavior and intricacies of the interaction in order to better understand the flow.

Another side benefit of the simulation is that many questions arise in the model development phase that relate to how the current operation is run. Any constraint or guideline that is questionable needs to be addressed and validated before taking it into consideration in the scheduling system. Only by closely examining different aspects of the operation can the modeler generate good recommendations and schedules.

The model-building team must be instructed not to take questions or criticism of the model personally. Such commentary is not an indication of the team's performance, but instead serves an important function in helping everyone to understand the flow more clearly. Inexperienced modelers can sometimes shy away from negativity, no longer asking important questions or validating the environment. It is best for the scheduling endeavor if these modelers persist through any discomfort and strive to improve everyone's knowledge of the operation.

HOW TO SCHEDULE EFFECTIVELY

Entire books could be written on how to schedule properly, but this section includes a few particularly important things to watch for.

First of all, **feedback** from the real-world system must be used as part of the scheduling system. For example, if a piece of equipment is running into efficiency problems, then the scheduling environment should take those delays into consideration and start scheduling around the problem until it is fixed.

This is valid in all industries. A **hospital** operating room may experience equipment problems that delay the start of a surgery, a **warehouse** fork truck may be running slower than usual or with less experienced workers, and a **manufacturing** environment may encounter maintenance issues in a piece of machinery.

Incorporating real-world information is also important when scheduling an automated system. If a piece of equipment is not running at its rated speed, and the system schedule is not modified, the bottleneck created quickly propagates throughout the system and generates extensive inefficiencies. On the other hand, automated systems have the capability to provide immediate feedback to the scheduling environment, and proper schedule sequencing can be modified accordingly.

As a rule, the scheduler should look at the main constraint of the system and develop a schedule around it regardless of the level of automation implemented. When a system is performing at the speed of its slowest process, proper scheduling must be maintained so that additional WIP is not created in order to increase the utilization of the rest of the operation. Creating more WIP to buffer the slowest operation is referred to the "Hurry Up and Wait" effect as it taxes part of the operation and increases space requirement, but adds no value to the overall efficiency and performance of the overall system. Scheduling to the slowest process, and propagating to the rest of the system, results in the most efficient environment based on the current constraints.

Note that as the live environment changes, the constraining process may migrate to different sections due to downtime, maintenance, or the manpower schedule; the schedule needs to be adjusted accordingly.

With a simulation model validated to represent the current environment, a generated schedule can be run on the simulation model to identify its effectiveness before sending it to the live system. This is another benefit of having a valid and updated model that is used beyond bottleneck analysis in order to improve and fine tune daily activities. For the schedule to be validated, it needs to load an initial state of the operation that represents the starting point for the schedule. Running a scheduler on an empty production environment leads to different results compared to when the machines are processing parts and entities are at different steps of the operation.

It is best for the scheduler to run on the current state of the operation. If the current state is not available, the schedule validation environment does not represent the true state of the operation and generates incorrect results.

One method used to avoid the current state loading scenario is to run the previous week's schedule first in order to preload the system with entities and components. In theory, and assuming that everything went as planned the previous week, the schedule validation is correct. Unfortunately, that rule doesn't always apply. The real-world environment has extensive variability in performance, which in turn renders this type of solution a semi-validation tool that only provides an idea of how the schedule performs.

One might argue that the current state is hard to retrieve and may not be 100% accurate. But in fact, most operating environments have an existing system that receives feedback on the progress and identifies the location of all the entities in the operation. These systems may not have detailed data on what the entity is doing at each station, but they do have information about the general location and size of the items, manpower, material handling, and any automation equipment that is running. In addition, scheduled maintenance and equipment changeover is already identified.

By collecting this data and entering it as the initial state of the simulation model, the schedule validation is more accurate. It is considered a valid representation of the real-world current state.

AUTOMATION

The addition of automation complicates the scheduling process. Furthermore, the need for humans to interface with the automated machinery requires more attention to detail and knowledge about the potential performance of the equipment.

In many cases, standard equipment performance is used, and when automated material handling is deployed, basic system averages are used to implement the schedule. Often, the results are inefficient schedules with expanded WIP that mask the true cause of the problem.

As a rule, if the schedule is generating WIP in order to support the flow, then the schedule is incomplete and inefficient. Keep in mind that WIP and cash flow are directly related. Any product that is being produced and is not shipped or delivered has an ownership cost associated with it and zero return. WIP is therefore expensive, and by reducing it, the cost of the operation decreases and cash flow increases. The goal of the scheduler should be to reduce WIP as much as possible without impacting the overall throughput of the system.

In automation, equipment operations are repetitive. Robots do the same task over and over again, always with the same precision and cycle time. They deviate from their standards when they need maintenance or fine tuning, and then they go back to their normal operations.

Guided vehicles are similar to other kinds of automation in that they have specific, repetitive tasks to perform. However, human interaction and the method of utilization impact their performance. If a guided vehicle needs to wait for a person to acknowledge or handle one of its items, then its performance is now related to the performance of the person and not just its own designed speed and efficiency. If the human interaction component is not taken into consideration, then the automated environment is rendered as inefficient as any other environment.

Another important consideration when it comes to automation is regular maintenance. Take for example the maintenance and charging cycles of guided vehicles. In general, a guided vehicle is battery operated and requires a consistent charge cycle in order for it to complete its tasks. The path of a guided vehicle may also vary depending on the assignment, and as controls for guided vehicles become more sophisticated, the guided vehicles are tasked with more missions that vary in distance, duration, and load capacity.

When the missions are not consistent across the system, scheduling the guided vehicles' charging cycle becomes more challenging. Many AGVs are charged based on a battery swap, in which the AGV goes to a battery changing station and the battery is replaced with a fresh, fully charged one. Another method uses an opportunity charging implementation, in which the AGV uses its non-active time (when a mission is not assigned) to charge its battery and maintain a healthy charging level.

When the mission requirement on the battery varies throughout the day, the discharge cycle of the battery also varies, and the time to perform opportunity charging becomes even more critical. In this case, the guided vehicle scheduler needs to even out the mission duration and battery stress across the fleet in order to minimize the impact.

For example, if a guided vehicle is used on long cycles, its battery depletes faster than the batteries in other vehicles and requires more charging time than the rest of the fleet, which reduces the operation's overall efficiency. Alternatively, if the load is evenly distributed, then the charging cycle is more manageable and better controlled.

Of course, the simulation environment helps in identifying the proper schedule for the AGVs as well as the number and type of charging required. In general, a battery swap system requires fewer AGVs than an opportunity charge system.

It is important to understand the capability and load on the material handling system. Overloading the transport system causes delays in moving items between locations and, in turn, slow down the overall throughput and render the schedule ineffective. Learning the limits of the material handling system is key to proper scheduling. This applies to both automated and manual material handling implementations.

It is important to identify the proper number of vehicles needed to transport and perform the tasks required. The presence of too many vehicles can lead to congestion and system delays, so adding material handling equipment is not always the best method to solve delays in transportation. One must use simulation to examine the logic and sequence of the system first. This strategy provides an understanding of the system's limits and options for improvement. Only after all other methods are exhausted would adding more vehicles to the fleet be a solution.

The same argument applies to all other automated systems. Take for example an **ASRS** that is capable of storing thousands of pallets in a concise and automated environment. The location of the stored items impacts the speed of storage and retrieval. The closer the item's location is to the load/unload position, the faster the item can be retrieved.

Moreover, storage that is more than a single item deep (multiple pallets stored in the same location in LIFO (Last in, First Out) implementation) impacts retrieval. Proper slotting of the ASRS becomes more important than its average operating speed and is heavily impacted by the schedule and the requests from the system.

Simulation can be used to study the schedule impact on the ASRS and figure out the best sequence to minimize re-slotting of the system. Re-slotting is performed when the ASRS starts to lose efficiency due to item locations and must perform internal movement to reorganize itself and regain its operational efficiency. Some ASRS systems attempt to perform a re-slot or pallet arrangement when no missions are assigned to it. Such systems are efficient and may improve the retrieval speed of the ASRS provided that it has enough knowledge on sequence of items to be retrieved.

Creating a schedule for any operation without a feedback loop from the real-world environment always leads to delays, bottlenecks, and missed orders. The fact is, without real-world feedback, the schedule is missing important information: the current state of the operation and all of its constraints.

Today's technology enables managers to receive data from all equipment using PLC connectivity, tracking material handling equipment using their locator devices, or any other entity, humans included, using passive or active RFID systems or similar technology. While all companies have this technology, not all of them use it in a meaningful way. Creating flashy dashboards to wow onlookers without putting the data set to use is a waste of time, effort, and money.

DYNAMIC SCHEDULING OF MATERIAL HANDLING EQUIPMENT

A useful scheduling system must be dynamic in a way that allows it:

- To react to the current state,
- Adjust its schedule based on real-life findings, and
- Push a modified schedule back to the operation.

If a problem occurs in the real-world environment that delays the schedule, there is always an alternative schedule that minimizes the delay until the problem is corrected. Instead of orders being delayed by two days, they may be delayed by only two hours. Instead of patients waiting for three hours, they may wait for 30 minutes. It all boils down to how quickly an operation can process its entities with the current conditions and goals.

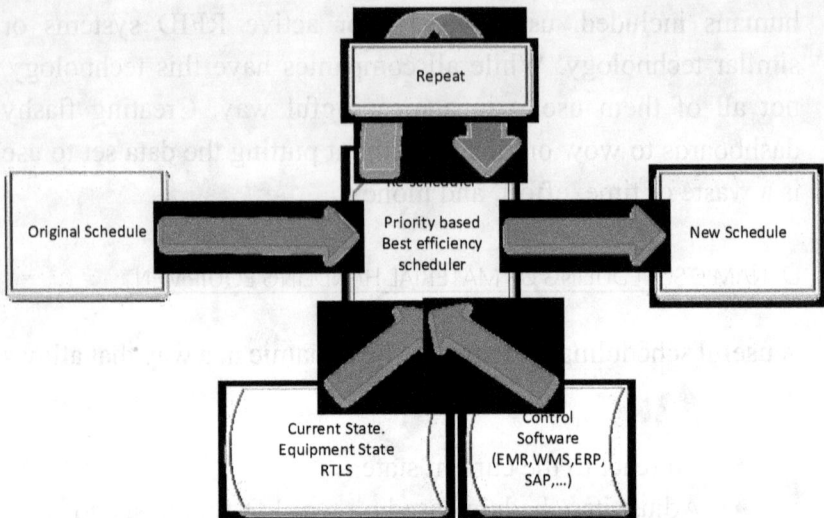

Image 11-1. Many factors should influence the creation of a new schedule. Schedule development should be an ongoing, dynamic process.

The scheduler needs to perform two main operations:

- Monitor the operation and identify when the schedule needs to be updated. These updates are triggered by a change in the real-world environment, new information from an external data set, or a detected future bottleneck that can be avoided.

- Generate and test the new schedule in a virtual background environment. If multiple schedules are possible, determine the best one to fit the operation, and send the new schedule back to the floor.

Of course, additional historical data and fine-tuning is required for the dynamic scheduler to work properly. Dynamic schedulers are complex, but tools exist to simplify and optimize the process. These tools are discussed in more detail in a later chapter.

To put things in perspective, let's examine a material handling scheduling scenario.

Normally, when **material handling** is required, most companies are interested in the number of units needed to perform the entity movement. In reality, the schedule and pickup/delivery requirement truly determine the number of units needed and how those units need to function in order to minimize their impact on the operation.

Material handling is a good example of scheduling analysis because material handling scenarios exist in every industry and most process flows.

In **healthcare**, material handling represents patient transport, replenishment of medicines to the floors and rooms, and surgical carts, among others. In **manufacturing** and automation, material handling represents all deliveries and movement within the operation requiring AGVs, fork lifts, or **Kanban** replenishment. In **warehousing** and supply chain management, material handling represents all pallet movement to storage, replenishment, picking, staging, and any other operation that requires entity movement.

Scheduling an operation's material handling is a common challenge, whether that operation is automated or manual. In most cases, this task is handled by adding material handling equipment instead of properly scheduling the operation. More equipment leads to increased congestion and safety concerns; this "solution" is ineffective.

The following diagram represents the material flow requirements (blue arrows) and requirements from the operational implementation. Requests to move entities within the operation are performed based on demand from each area. Material handling equipment (MHE) are used to move in and out of each zone while avoiding the blocked areas. Required distances and speeds vary depending on the path taken, with some congestion that can exist in each zone and along the route.

Image 11-2. Block flow diagram for MHE scheduling.

The true question here is this: are we scheduling the MHE to fit the operation, or scheduling the operation and hoping the MHE can keep up and handle the load? Most operations schedule the operation and assume that the MHE is able to pick up the volume and deliver on time. This assumption does not always match reality.

Another important factor to consider is the number and location of charging stations. Location choices may create unexpected delays into the operation. In the model above, there is one area for charging and maintenance. Depending on the amount of traffic going to different zones, it may be beneficial to add more charging stations, but this decision should be driven by the schedule and the "need to charge" the MHE.

Before addressing any strategies to identify the proper scheduling method and sequencing required for the operation, it is important to first consider the constraints of the system. These constraints should be examined in three steps.

First, for each process (equipment, interface, resource, and so on), identify the limits and list them in priority order. Include in this list all perceived limits from the providers running the operation. All identified items should be listed, per process, regardless of the number of occurrences.

Second, identify the effect of each limit on the process flow as it is perceived in the current operation. These effects may include quality issues, equipment performance, downstream delays, product sequencing, picking constraints, or flow constraints, to name a few. The goal in this exercise is to identify all of the constraints used in today's (or the proposed future) scheduling method.

Third, consider whether or not each imposed limit is needed. Validate and question these limitations based on their role in the analyzed environment. For example, there might have been some historical use of specific components (e.g. first product A, then product B) that required the products to be sequenced in a set way. Depending on the history of the operation, changes may have occurred that now render this sequencing order unnecessary for the current process.

While one must be careful not to eliminate items that are quality-related before discussing the implementation change with the appropriate departments, one must also consider whether the constraints have a purpose in the process as it exists now. Consider: is that requirement (first product A, then product B) still necessary in the new system? If it is, what is the impact of the requirement on the effect of the limits?

Entity	Limit Description	Effect	Is it Needed?
Press Machine	Setup required after each job		
	Maintenance required daily at 10am		
	Requires 2 resources to operate		
	Jobs have to be sequenced in a specific order		

Table 11-1. A sample examination of system constraints.

After the table is complete, the constraints and limits should be migrated to a simulation model that represents the flow. In our case, each of the zones generates a request for MHE in order to complete its tasks. The goal of the simulation model is to understand the effect of the limits on the operation and their impact on the overall throughput of the system.

The above table should now be expanded to include the effect of the limits using an existing schedule. Therefore, the model needs to load an already developed schedule (if it is a new operation, a random made-up schedule can be used), and define the impact of each of the limits in a scenario set analysis. Only by running the model in this way can the true impact of the limits be identified and documented.

Once the effects of the limits have been identified, determine the limits that have the largest impact and examine the reason for their occurrence. For example, one might notice that certain limits are imposed on the system based on the schedule itself and the way it is formed. These limits can be avoided in future scheduling methods. After all of the unnecessary limits are identified and removed from the list, the modeler needs to identify the MHE request sequences.

When we examine the implementation flow, it is easy to notice that not all paths are equal. From the simulation model, the modeler can identify the number of required requests to and from each zone.

The simplest implementation, and the one that requires the most MHE units, is to segment the load and dedicate MHE units to each set of transfers. Then use simple math to identify the number needed. If Zone 1 sends items to Zone 4 every 15 minutes and there is a 5 minute travel time between zones each way, then as long as the MHE can load and unload the unit in 5 minutes, 1 MHE is needed for that type of transfer. The same can be applied to other zone transfers and a total number of necessary MHE units can be identified.

There are two issues with such an implementation. First, congestion through the aisles and at the stations is not taken into consideration. Second, it tends to overstate the number of MHE units to perform the tasks. Furthermore, if any charging and maintenance is required for the MHE units, then the number required doubles. The problem is compounded if the MHE is only assigned a task when it is at the home position, as this option creates additional travel that would otherwise be unnecessary.

The modeler's choices should now be driven by three main factors.

1. Reduce the number of MHEs to eliminate aisle congestion.
2. Synchronize the MHE movements in order to minimize empty travel. (Empty travel occurs when the MHE is traveling without an entity being transferred.)
3. Identify when a new MHE request is handled and which MHE supports the request.

When using the simulation model, the modeler needs to assume that there is one MHE fleet that can be assigned to do any task within the operation. When a request for entity movement is made at each of the zones, the MHE scheduler needs to first identify the time constraint to handle the request. Just because the request is made does not mean that it needs to be handled immediately, as there might be other more urgent movements required. That decision is made based on the zone schedules and the buffer availability at each zone.

In addition, a move cannot be started until it is known that the entity can be dropped off at its destination without delays. Otherwise, the MHE system is used as an expensive dynamic buffer.

With these rules in mind, the following needs to occur before an MHE unit is assigned:

1. There is a need for the entity to move based on the zone schedule

2. There is an MHE available to make the move that does not disrupt a higher priority move
3. There is a position available at the destination location

If the move is not immediately assigned, it should be included in a "request queue" that is handled when the MHE system is available to make the move.

The MHE scheduling system must assign a new task every time the MHE becomes available, and it must do so without proceeding to a home destination. The simulation model helps to determine if the MHE should wait at the last drop-off position, proceed to its next potential location based on the zone schedule (and preferably real-time feedback), or go to the home position or charging station.

Charging and maintenance requirements cannot be overlooked. This requirement might look like a command to send the MHE to a charging station for ten minutes every hour, for example.

Note that in an environment with highly variable travel paths (similar to this implementation), staggering the start of the MHE does not solve the sequencing issue that results from MHE charging. In other words, due to the dynamics of such system, and if charging is required on an hourly basis, the depletion rate and the time of charge is the main constraint of the system. These limitations eventually need to be synchronized so that most of the MHE fleet requires charging at the same time. Careful scheduling of the MHE paths in each zone can help the modeler determine the ideal time to charge and decide if multiple charging stations are necessary. Additional charging constraints may also be identified such as pre-emptive charging in order to maximize the use of the AGVs and allow them to charge when they're idle even if their charge replenishment level is not reached.

RECAP

Scheduling is a complicated endeavor that ultimately plays a large role in the efficiency of any operation. The challenges inherent in scheduling can be daunting, but simulation modeling can help an operation to reach its full potential by providing insight into the different arrangements available.

By scheduling the MHE units correctly, connecting their schedules to the zone schedule, and receiving feedback from the actual environment, it is possible to reduce the number of MHEs used by 50%, all while keeping the system in check and reducing congestion and movement across the facility.

The key is to have an environment that can analyze the current state and accurately project the potential future state based on known parameters. As systems become more complex and automated, the need for dynamic real-time schedulers becomes critical in making sure the operation runs at its maximum efficiency.

The following chapters address industry-specific applications of simulation modeling by considering a sample scenario and addressing it through each of the simulation-building steps discussed in earlier chapters.

Chapter 12: Simulation in Healthcare

This chapter covers a complete simulation project of a surgical center and discusses the initial findings, model building stages, analytics, and optimization. Although the presented method covers a surgical center, the method can be applied to all aspects of healthcare including emergency departments, clinics, imaging facilities, and others.

(If the hospital *supply chain* is being simulated and improved, it is better to follow the methods in the warehousing model detailed in a later chapter with slight variation based on the fact that the distribution is within a hospital.)

The healthcare industry, particularly in a surgical setting, faces a wide variety of challenges and very high stakes. Coordinating doctors, nurses, patients, cleaning staff, carts, and locations would be difficult enough on its own, but the added variability of timing due to unexpectedly long or complex operations makes it even more difficult to schedule with confidence.

Despite these challenges, there are changes that can be made to alleviate some of the burdens that a typical surgical center faces. Check-in procedures, architectural planning, and the arrangement of rooms and resources, for example, can all be scheduled and laid out properly. Those changes can lead to significant results: reduced length of stay, increased bed availability, improved quality of care, and higher patient satisfaction.

The inter-related processes of a healthcare setting creates a complicated system and dynamic environment that can be challenging to predict, schedule and optimize. This includes the dynamics of patients, doctors, nurses, and other staff members, coupled with system and case variability. Oftentimes, when working toward improving individual aspects of the operation, it is difficult to identify the impact of a change on other areas, as well as on the system as a whole. Each change has far-reaching consequences, sometimes in areas one might not expect.

For this reason, static analysis tools such as Microsoft Excel® often fail to make accurate predictions. Static analysis simply cannot keep tabs on the complex process relationships that are a hospital's daily reality. Running a surgical center based on averages provides average results that fail to identify where improvement should take place and how it should be implemented.

Dynamic simulation allows for the relationship between entities to be maintained. This is one of the most important parts of a hospital setup. It also creates an immersive and interactive scenario development and opportunity testing environment. The user can interact with the virtual environment and test, "on-the-fly," any and all changes to layout, processes, patients, medical staff, scheduling, etc. These tests allow the user to examine what changes have a positive impact on the operation without entering into a risky real-life trial and error period.

DEFINING THE PROBLEM

In this scenario, the location in question is a surgical center. This surgical center may or may not be in a hospital setting. The center has the main constraints that any surgical center would have: a front desk for check-in, a waiting room, a set of pre-op and post-op beds, and a number of dedicated surgical rooms that need to be controlled. Each bed needs to be cleaned after patient use.

Every surgical room needs to be cleaned, supplied with necessary items, staffed with medical providers, and occupied by a patient before a surgery can start. Furthermore, patient transport must be handled according to proper procedures and should not impact the surgical center efficiency.

The model needs to address some of the key questions for the center, such as:

- What is the maximum capacity of the center?
- What type of scheduling do we use? (Block, hybrid, or other?)
- How do we best schedule the center?
- Does the supply chain of surgical carts have an impact on the schedule?
- How many providers are needed, and what is the impact of provider delays on the overall schedule?
- Is transport a problem? Would it create a bottleneck if the center increases its capacity?
- How should we allocate pre-op and post-op beds? Should they be combined or should they be separated?

Aside from these questions, there are also standard questions in a medical setting: should we add more surgical rooms? What type should they be? How would that addition impact the rest of the system?

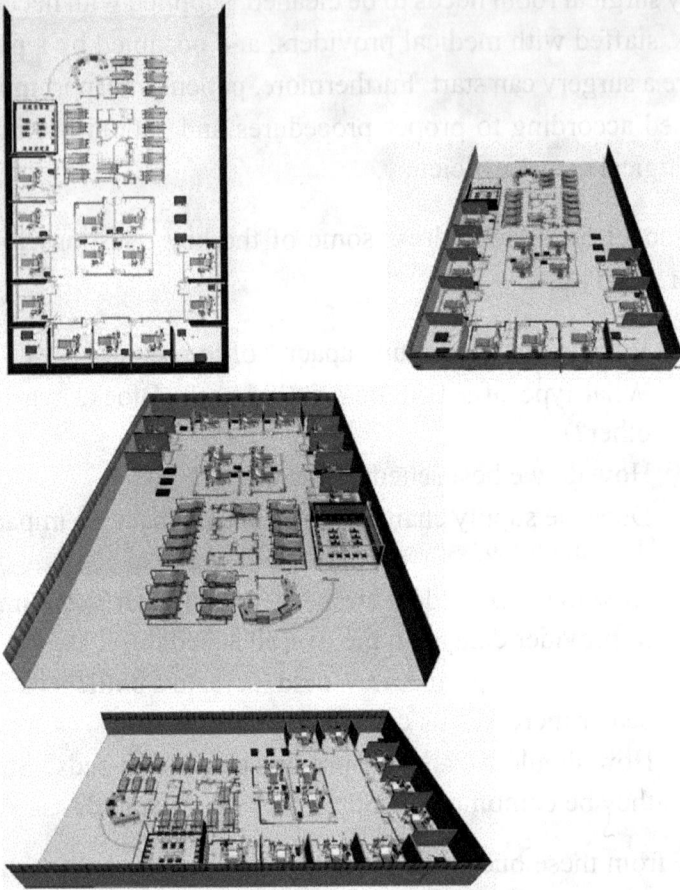

Image 12-1. Basic surgical center model.

The treatment cycle for patients is to enter the surgical center, be checked in by the receptionist, and wait in the waiting room until they are called in for pre-op. The patient is then brought to an open bed, prepared for surgery by a nurse (or nursing staff, surgeons, anesthesiologist, or other appropriate medical provider), and moved into an operating room once it is available. A surgeon operates on the patient, and then the patient is returned to the post-op bed for recovery and the operating room is cleaned.

After the recovery period, the patient is either free to leave or needs to be admitted to the hospital.

Of course, a lot of detail is left out of this description. Each part of the cycle requires multiple provider interactions, multiple steps and, of course, the surgical carts full of supplies. In order to answer all of the above questions, the full model needs to be expanded and all details implemented. However, some questions can be answered while constructing the basic model. The key is to create enough of the model in order to address the initial key questions.

GOAL-SETTING

As discussed earlier, the team must first identify the goals of the simulation project and determine the priority of each goal. Based on the current requirements and the above questions to be answered, the team's goals should look something like the following list:

- Identify the maximum capacity of the center, assuming unlimited surgical carts, unlimited providers, and combining pre-op and post-op beds to use them as a group allocation.
- Identify the impact of providers on the capacity models. How many providers are needed to achieve maximum capacity, and what capacity can be achieved with the currently allocated teams and providers? Study the impact of transport on the center and identify any potential bottlenecks and the number of transport constraints.
- Identify the impact of the supply room and surgical cart availability on the operation. Can the supply chain support an increase in capacity? What limits would the

supply carts impose on the efficiency and capacity of the center? The simulation model identifies the optimum flow from the supply room in order to eliminate any potential surgical delays.

- Last, identify how different schedules improve the operation. Is block scheduling or a hybrid model better suited to the center's needs? Is it better to implement an open schedule? How many surgical rooms should be allocated to specific surgery types, and can some of them be combined in order to maximize efficiency and utilization of each room?

In order to accomplish these goals, the model-building process follows three phases.

- Phase 1 is the construction of the basic model.
- Phase 2 is to add resource constraints.
- Phase 3 is to increase the amount of detail present in the sub-flows and incorporate surgical carts in a true-to-life manner.

DATA COLLECTION

Before creating the model, the team collects information. In this particular case, the team should collect data regarding:

- The number of beds available in the pre- and post-op location
- The size of the waiting room and any available floor plans of the surgical center
- Cycle times for the various types of procedures

This category includes not only the different surgeries, but also check-in, pre-op, sanitization and cleaning of the operating room, nurse checks on the patients, physician examinations for discharge, and any other procedure necessary to the process flow.

Historical and anticipated patient volumes by surgery type. If the surgical center has seasonal surgery type fluctuations, then each season's metrics will have to be captured.

All of the above information will be useful in the first phase of constructing the basic model. In pursuit of the future goals regarding resource availability, the team also collects data about the staff and other resources.

For example: How many doctors and nurses are there? What are their specialties and skill sets? How many cleaning staff members are there? How many surgical carts are there? Collecting data about resources is not relevant to the capacity analysis, but it is necessary to achieve the team's future goals.

PHASE 1: CONSTRUCTION OF BASIC MODEL

The surgical center (Image 12-1 above) consists of a waiting section and 3 stages: pre-operation, surgery, and post-operation. In order to achieve the first simulation analysis goal, the team needs to implement the relationships between the different process steps, identify the cycle time distribution (or actuals for each), and load the patient data set to drive the model.

The implementation of the model should follow the basic flow of the process:

- Patient comes in,
- Waits in the waiting room until a pre-op bed is available,
- Gets assigned a surgical room,
- Proceeds to a post-op bed, then
- Leaves the center.

Some simulation tools can implement a modular building method that allows a single change to propagate through the model. In such an environment, the modeler needs to define three different modules, one for the surgical room, one for the waiting room, and one for the pre/post-op rooms then apply those to the different processes. Adding a new surgical room later based on the module would ensure that all properties and logic are properly set.

With the processes defined at individual stations, the team creates the path that the patient (and later, providers and carts) will travel through. The model-building process is highly dependent on which type of simulation tool is used. Some tools require an extensive web of connections for different entities, while others create paths that entities can travel through.

The following image represents the completed simulation model.

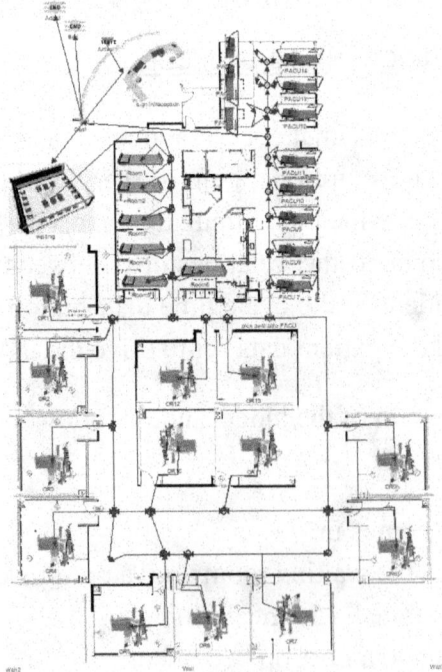

Image 12-2. Simulation model with basic process flow.

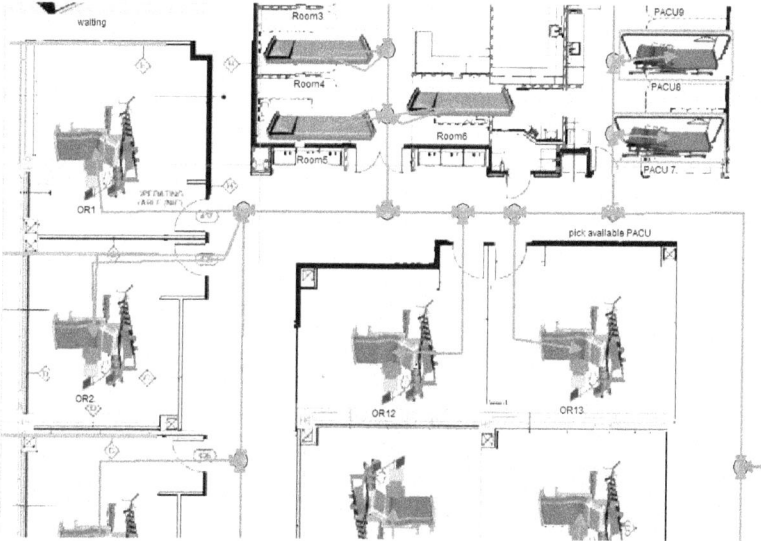

Image 12-3. Hallways/paths are identified in orange. Each path can be single or bi-directional depending on flow constraints.

For the model to be tested, the model must animate the flow of patients through the center. This feature is another aspect of a simulation tool that can greatly impact the model development speed.

If the animation is separate from the model building and paths that have been defined, then model development turnaround time will suffer, and modeling will take longer to complete. In contrast, more advanced tools provide direct animation based on the defined flow (such as the tool used in this example, Simcad Process Simulator). Therefore, the model is ready to animate and run the simulation based on an input data set.

In order to provide the best implementation for the pre- and post-op room, the modeler implements a routing method out of the waiting room to the least busy pre-op bed. As long as there is a pre-op bed available, a patient is sent to that bed for surgery. The same behavior is implemented after the surgery is complete, and an available post-op bed is used for the patient.

Note that we are not basing pre/post-op allocation based on acuity or other factors. These early model-building steps are purely an exercise to determine the maximum capacity possible for the surgical center based on the timing characteristics provided. After post-op, patients are either sent home (65% for example) or required to be admitted to the hospital (35%), which requires an additional transport.

During this initial model construction, the team also adds a reception desk and a waiting room area in the front. This addition allows a queue to form as a buffer in case there is an overflow of patients.

After building the model, team members add metrics to determine the usage of each room and how many patients are completed.

"Chapter 7: Expanding the Model and Adding Detail" discussed the importance of adding hooks in the basic model that can later be used to expand it. In this case, the hook is the fact that each room or bed will become a sub-flow. Building the model with the plan of eventually expanding single processes into sub-flows is a sufficient hook in this case.

Because the team will later add resources such as healthcare providers, cleaners, and surgical carts to the sub-flow, there is no need to include those resources at this stage. Instead, team members should set aside the resource question for now and assume that the necessary resources are already present whenever the surgery needs to start.

PHASE 1A: VALIDATION

The team bases its validation on historical comparison. Team members load the model with four different sets of actual data collected from recent history. These data sets vary to represent the seasonality and heavy/light schedules for the operating rooms. Each data set identifies a patient's arrival time (check-in), time spent in pre-op, wheels in/wheels out time of surgery, and time spent in post-op. The model will use the loaded data set either to create a distribution, or to run based on actual data and compare the final results with actuals.

If actuals are used, the model results should match the real-world throughput and utilization, as this is, in fact, a replay of all events that occurred in the actual environment. Therefore model validation can be performed quickly with a high degree of accuracy.

The next step is to create a set of distributions for surgery time and arrival rate for the patients. The surgery time needs to be applied based on surgery type, not an overall number for all surgeries. In addition, the breakdown of arriving patients based on surgery type can be computed and applied.

After the distributions are created, a set of Monte Carlo runs need to be made to ensure the consistency and accuracy of the model based on the current data set. The model should, for the most part, maintain the accuracy of its results, provided that it ran long enough to eliminate any potential outliers that may exist in the distributed environment.

PHASE 1B: ANALYSIS

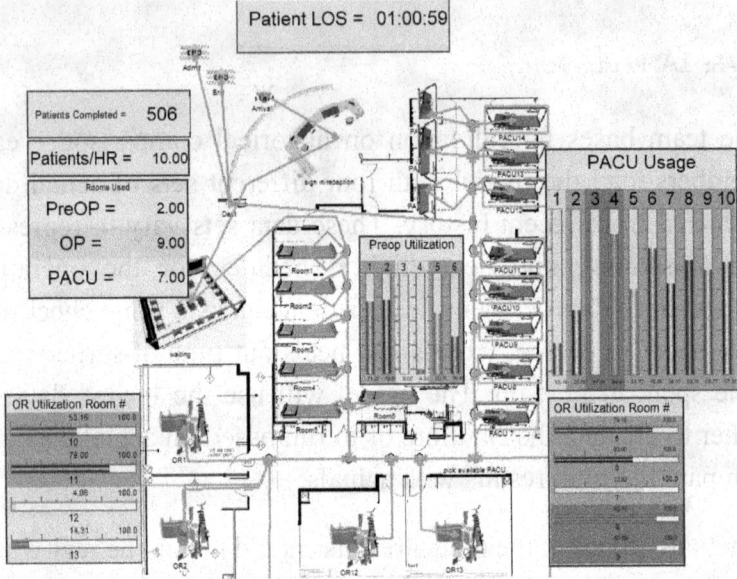

Image 12-4. Basic surgical center analytics.

The analysis goal for this phase is to determine the theoretical maximum number of patients the surgical center can process in eight hours. To accomplish this goal, the team conducts two tests: first, a test to see how many patients can complete the process in an eight-hour shift, and second, a test to see how long it takes to complete 200 patients.

The results are below.

	Test 1	Test 2
Length of Time	8 hours	2 days, 5:53:32
Patients Completed	44	200

Length of Stay	55:30	42:29
Admitted / Home	30 / 14	125 / 75

Table 12-0-1 Maximum number of patients the surgical center can process in eight hours.

These results indicate that with absolutely no constraints the surgical center can process 44 patients in an eight-hour shift. That means there's no need to clean the rooms, everyone arrives on time, there are unlimited doctors and nurses as needed, etc.

While this number is obviously unattainable in real life, finding the theoretical maximum helps the surgical center staff to plan ahead. If, for example, the surgical center manager wants to process 45 patients in every eight-hour shift, perhaps renovations need to be made to the surgical center to build more operating suites.

To determine a slightly more realistic goal, the team also adds a room cleaning reprocessing feature to the model and performs the same tests. The results of those tests are below.

	Test 1	Test 2
Length of Time	8 hours	2 days, 5:48:44
Patients Completed	22	200
Length of Stay	49:45	51:23
Admitted / Left	8 / 14	129 / 71

Table 12-0-2 Maximum number of patients the surgical center can process in eight hours with room cleaning reprocessing feature

These results provide valuable information: room cleaning cuts down considerably on the number of patients that can be seen in an eight-hour shift. This lower target of 22 patients is a more realistic one that the surgical center managers should strive for. Note that there is a limit imposed on the model in relation to the number of cleaning room crew that is available and the number of rooms that can be cleaned at the same time. In this case, the model assumes an unlimited number of simultaneous room cleanings possible, and the only real change in the model is the availability of the surgical room for the next patient.

It is important to note that in this phase, all surgical rooms are considered equal and the only difference is the duration of the procedure. Therefore, the model again assumes maximum availability of the rooms and no impact on room capability or scheduling constraints. By opening up the surgery room to a wide variety of surgery types, a true theoretical maximum can be achieved, which is the main goal of this phase.

Additional Monte Carlo runs show the consistency of the model:

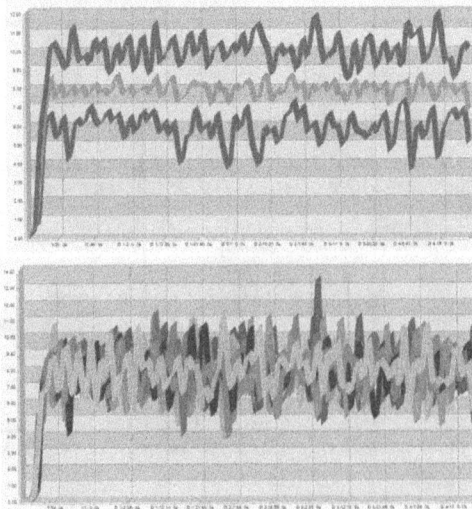

Image 12-5. Patient rate/hour. The image on the top shows min/max/average. The image on the bottom shows the actual data.

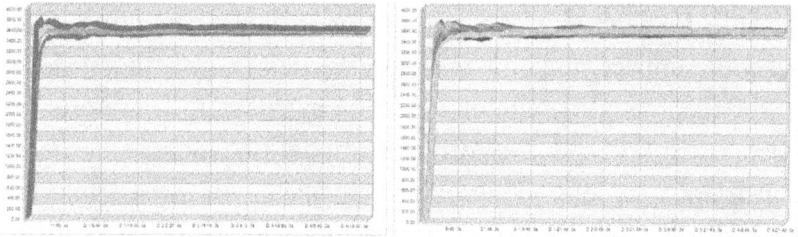

Image 12-6. Length of stay identified in seconds. The image in the left shows min/max/average. The image on the right shows the actual data.

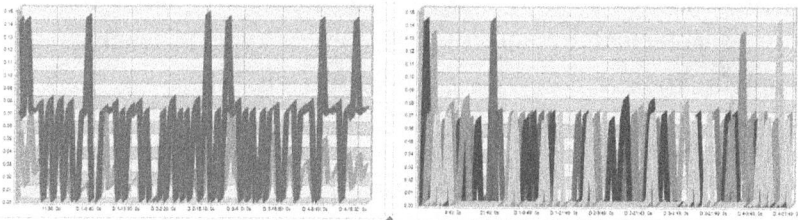

Image 12-7. Waiting room capacity.

PHASE 1C: OPTIMIZATION

This phase, in which a basic model is built to perform a capacity analysis, does not require any optimization effort. Optimization will take place in later phases.

PHASE 2: ADD RESOURCE CONSTRAINTS

The main goal of the second phase is to understand the impact of providers on the surgical center. Based on that, the modeler will be able to determine the number of providers required, their schedule impact, and how many are needed in order to get closer to the theoretical maximum achieved in Phase 1. Therefore, the goal is to expand the original model to include resource constraints so that a resource analysis can be performed. Specifically, this phase examines the role of people: nurses, doctors, transports, and cleaning staff.

Since the cleaning process was already introduced in Phase 1, the modeler needs to apply a resource requirement to that object type so that it cannot start unless the resource is present. In Simcad, this is achieved by selecting the object type "Cleaning" and applying the resource "Cleaning Staff" to it.

The actual provider movement within the center is already identified through hallways defined in Phase 1, so the modeler simply needs to let the resource travel based on a specific speed and allow the simulation environment to figure out the best path of travel from room-to-room. In order to identify the path to the destination, the simulation tool should be able to automatically compute potential paths and distances to the destination and determine the shortest path of least resistance unless a specific path is required. Since this is a native feature of Simcad, the model behavior change for the cleaning resource is complete.

Additional resources for the transport provider need to be set up for the movement of the patient. The model constraint indicates that for the patient to move from pre-op to the operating room and out to post-op, the transport needs to be present. The transport paths, earlier identified as hallways, will now require the transport resource in order to move the patient throughout the center. The change, then, is to modify the module defined for the path and add the transport to the patient.

Last, the modeler needs to expand the interaction between the patient and providers in all three areas of the center. The interaction will vary by procedure and needs to be implemented without modifying the original model. Therefore, there is a need for three separate treatment flows (or sub-flows) identifying the detailed interaction between patient and provider: one for pre-op, one for the surgery room, and one for post-op.

Three different sub-flows will be implemented, one for each process flow. Later on, the process flows can be separated based on case or surgery type, but for the current goal requirement, only a single sub-flow per processing type is needed.

The pre-op process includes getting the patient to the room, prepping the patient, collecting vitals, another nurse check, an anesthesiologist visit, a surgeon visit, and multiple nurse visits until the surgical room is available. For each of the above steps, a cycle time is entered and a resource (provider) requirement is assigned.

The last step is to define the pre-op process to run the pre-op sub-flow when the patient is activated. From this point forward, all changes to the pre-op sub-flow are applied to all pre-op beds. Furthermore, different variations of the pre-op process flow can be implemented in the sub-flow itself. By repeating the process for the surgical room and the post-op beds, the model is ready for another round of validation before the analysis begins.

PHASE 2A: VALIDATION

If the model is built with the simulation running, the model expansion and flow validation will already be complete at this time. When other non-interactive modeling environments are used instead, a complete process flow and constraints validation needs to be completed, much like Phase 1A Validation.

The results of the model should be validated based on the available historical data. By loading the same set of data as was used in Phase 1, the model should behave and generate similar results to the ones received when the number of providers exceeds their constraints requirement.

In other words, set the number of providers to be much higher than the model needs, thereby eliminating the resource constraints, and then run the model. This validation will ensure that the model is valid from a capacity perspective. Next, enter the actual number of resources available in the real-world system and perform a full simulation run. The model results should now be compared to actuals; it should be within 1% of the actual data set.

The difference between the validation of the basic model and validation in the following phases is that each time, 1) the team validates the original data first, *then* 2) adds to it the validation of new changes. That way, the team can guarantee that the original model is still valid before testing any new changes.

PHASE 2B: ANALYSIS AND OPTIMIZATION

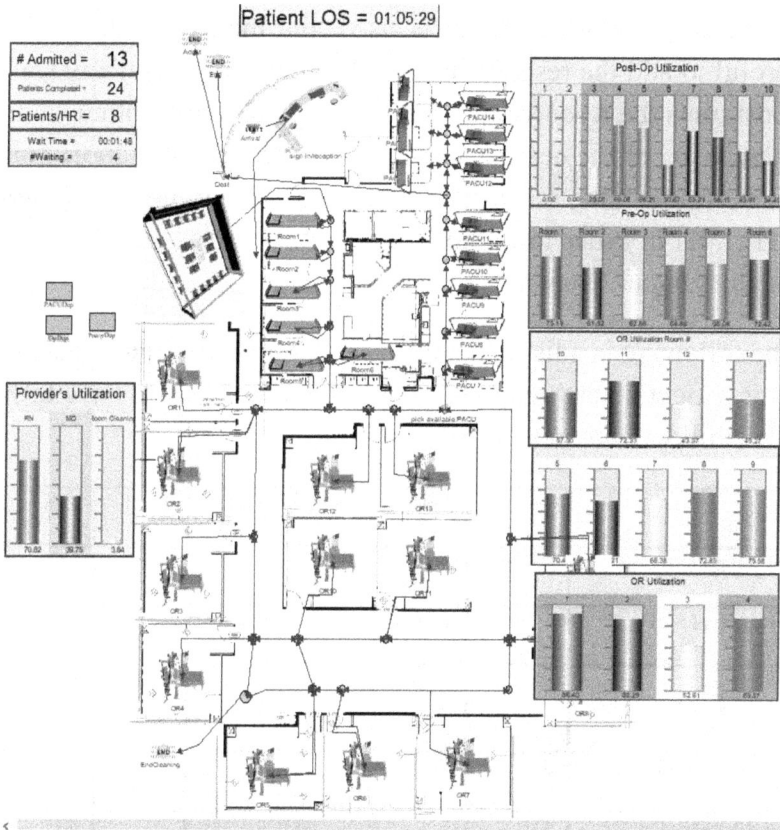

Image 12-8. Resource analytics with sub-flows (or treatment flows).

The goal for this phase is to determine the optimal number of resources required to run the current load with maximum efficiency, and the total number of resources required to run at maximum capacity. One option is for the modeling team to a) employ an optimizer that learns from the system behavior (for example, based on a neural network), b) generate the required results, and c) validate them on the model.

228

Another method to determine the resource requirement is to make a number of simulation runs with different provider numbers and availability. If an optimizer is used, the modeler needs to be careful to add the resource availability percentage and any shift constraints the resource might have; otherwise, the optimization exercise is only a guess regarding what is needed. If multiple runs are performed, the scenarios can implement varying availability and shifts in order to minimize the number of resources while maximizing utilization.

The following is a list of sample runs for an 8 hour duration and their patient/hour throughput. All providers are set to have 80% availability in the model.

	Test 1	Test 2	Test 3	Test 4	Test 5	Test 6
Total patient count	19	17	22	4	11	22
Length of Stay	1:43:56	1:25:40	1:21:41	3:03:58	2:18:40	1:21:33
#Admitted / Discharged	12 / 7	10 / 7	14 / 8	4 / 0	3 / 8	15 / 7
# MD Available	3	5	6	3	3	3
# RN Available	3	3	6	1	2	4
# Cleanup Resources	1	3	5	3	3	2

Table 12-3 Sample runs for 8-hour duration and patient/hour throughput

Based on the generate results, the team determines that there must be at least 2 nurses present for the model to run at a steady rate. Tests 3 and 6, in which the number of nurses was greater than or equal to the number of doctors, provided the optimal results, achieving 22 patients seen—the same number as the theoretical maximum when cleaning was implemented in the first phase.

PHASE 3: INCREASE DETAILS

The third phase of model implementation expands the model to add surgical carts to the process. Prior to the start of each surgical procedure, a certain number of surgical carts needs to be delivered to the operating room. The number of carts delivered depends on the type of surgery being performed, but the surgery cannot start until all necessary carts are available. The model assumes that the delivered surgical cart is the correct one as it is outside of the scope of the model to analyze the impact of an incorrect cart being delivered.

For the model to be complete, the surgical cart process needs to include:

- The time to prepare the carts and
- The transfer of the carts to the surgical area.

A set of resources needs to be identified in the cart preparation area, and a dedicated transport must be assigned to move the cart to its appropriate destination based on the current schedule.

In addition, the cart transport needs to remove all used carts from the operating room and move them back for cleaning and sanitizing before delivering the next set of carts. The distance and path traveled by the cart become a critical part of the surgical center performance. After all, the longer the travel distance, the longer it takes to deliver and remove the carts.

As the cart arrives at a surgical room process, it enters the sub-flow, so all interaction and waiting is performed with the sub-flow. During this interaction, the top level model does not change, and neither do any other parts of the model, including pre-op and post-op stations, patient movement, and patient arrivals. The only part that needs to be modified is the section relating to the use of the surgical cart.

PHASE 3A: VALIDATION

Since the only part that changed in the model is the surgical cart flow and its impact on the operating room, only that section needs to be validated. The modeler needs to make sure that the carts are going to the proper rooms and following the correct path. At this point, an entity-based spaghetti diagram would help in validating the flow of each of the components of the model.

PHASE 3B: ANALYSIS

The first analysis step is to verify the impact of the surgical carts on the system. What are the limits for cart delivery? What type of impact do the surgical carts have, and how can the team eliminate any impact of the cart delivery on the overall operation of the surgical center?

The key is to run the existing patient arrival pattern and verify that the number of patients treated is the same as in the model without the carts. Once the baseline for the model is defined, the modeler needs to reduce the number of resources assigned to the cart delivery and identify the minimum number required to maintain the current operation while, at the same time, determining the impact of the lack of resources.

Identifying the proper schedule to allocate the surgical room or combining pre- and post-op will require some changes, but these alterations can be performed similarly to earlier changes in the model.

Admittedly, managing a hybrid schedule can be a bit tricky. Optimizing it and identifying the number of surgeries required per type in order to maximize either of the schedulers can be even more complex. It requires more analysis and understanding of the model. Both operations can be completed based on the current model implementation. In fact, many simulation models have been implemented to perform the schedule optimization task.

RECAP

As this hypothetical surgical center model demonstrates, simulation modeling serves a useful and important purpose in optimizing the flow of a healthcare operation.

Interactive simulation software can have a profound effect on hospital efficiency. It is more straightforward. Faster to build than software that requires extensive coding. And it can adapt better to changes made on the fly.

This kind of software can examine layout and relationships between different elements of the process. It can identify problem areas and predict future circumstances in order to better prepare the hospital staff members for the patients they encounter.

When deciding whether to buy a new piece of simulation software, don't be afraid to ask questions. Here are some sample questions that may shed light on different aspects and capabilities of simulation software:

- How do I go about making changes to the system?
- Do I have to stop the model every time I want to make a change? Can you show me how that can be accomplished with a fresh model?

- From a new model, can I see the analysis and comparison between current and future states?
- How can I account for the variability in patient types and arrival times?
- Is it possible to quickly expand the current model and add detail without disturbing the current implementation?

These questions and many others can contribute to a greater understanding of what benefits certain software may be able to provide. Hospitals and surgical centers are increasingly expected to stretch their resources and do more with less. It is imperative to understand the differences in simulation software so that team members can choose the best possible software for their needs.

Chapter 13: Simulation in a Distribution Center

Achieving a high level of efficiency in distribution centers (DC) is a constantly changing target for all DC managers and process improvement managers.

Distribution centers, in general, have a very basic functionality: they receive goods, store them, then stage and deliver them to end users and customers. Optimizing and efficiently running a warehouse may seem, to a novice, like a simple and straightforward operation.

In reality, managing warehouses to perform efficiently is one of the most complex tasks that a manager can face. A 1-second delay in delivery can easily become a huge loss in operational efficiency when compounded over the thousands of items that the warehouse manages.

Many companies have opted for extensive automation to improve warehousing, including ASRS, STVs and AGVs, robots, and automated smart conveyors. However, warehouses still face inefficiencies that stem sometimes from the very basic implementation of automation and other from operational inefficiencies.

Automation, when designed properly, can and will improve the efficiency of the warehouse. Yet in many cases it fails to provide the required efficiency improvement and, in some cases, is the cause of the efficiency degradation.

This chapter explores a set of simulation methods that will help in designing an efficient warehouse or improve the efficiency of an existing one. It is important to note that a warehouse is not a constant entity, but an ever-changing environment that is impacted by outside factors, internal operational changes, and a large number of items that need to be stored, maintained and shipped.

Before going into details of the implementation, each distribution center consists of certain common functionalities, including:

The ability to receive large quantities of items. Some are sorted by item type, while others are not. Each item needs to be identified by its properties and characteristics and stored in known locations in order to simplify retrieval.

A racking system to store the received items until they are needed for shipping is required. The racking system needs to be properly slotted in order to reduce the amount of travel required to retrieve the items in bulk either for picking or for direct shipment. Regardless whether the storage system is automatic or not, properly organizing the location of each item type in the storage system is critical to the overall efficiency of the warehouse.

A "Rack to Picking" transfer operation may be required in some distribution centers. In the case where picking is performed on a small subset of the stored items, or to maintain a large number of stored items, picking may be performed in an optimized picking area instead of picking directly from racks.

The operation of picking items from specific location based on specific orders is the picking environment of the warehouse. There may be a dedicated picking area present or picking may occur directly from the racks. In general, the dedicated picking environment usually serves as a high speed picking system due to the reduction of travel to a pick face and the position of the pick location with respect to the picking system. The picking system may involve different picking technologies such as pick to cart, zone picking, baker's cart picking, and others.

As items are picked, the quantities in the pick front is reduced and has to be replenishment from storage, this is the replenishment system. Each distribution center maintains a set of rules to replenish the pick area, regardless of the picking environment. If picking is performed directly from racks low level positions, a replenishment from top location to bottom locations may be needed. On the other hand, when replenishment is performed to a dedicated picking area, replenishment will require material and item movement from storage racks to the picking environment.

As items and orders are picked, they need to be organized together for shipment to their destination, this is the staging and shipping environment. Staging and shipping is a dedicated section of the warehouse for grouping picked items together and directing them to a proper shipping lane for final delivery to the end user. The extensiveness of the staging area depends on the type of picking performed. It can vary based on the implementation and may require extensive sorting and grouping which can be performed manually, with automation or as a combination of both. Based on the above requirements, a distribution center needs to process known items to a certain extent that has constant variability in the way items are received, stored, processed, picked and delivered. Seasonality, delayed delivery, internal operations, and other factors contribute to the complexity of the distribution center and the challenges it faces in maintaining a highly efficient operation.

The goal of improving distribution center efficiency is to reduce the time and handling required for each received and shipped item. Reducing the number of touches required to control an item reduces the number of errors and makes the internal operation more predictable.

An important factor in measuring efficiency is the amount of handling of items that are not required for shipping. For example, pulling a pallet down from a rack just to pick one item then putting it back on the rack is excessive handling and should be avoided. Another example would be performing a replenishment task for an item that is not needed in the next set of picking cycles while other items need to be replenished and are to be picked next.

In order to improve efficiency, many companies have opted to implement highly automated systems to reduce the human factor and introduce more consistency in the internal operation. These systems, which seem like a good choice in principle, rarely produce to their potential and most often fail to meet their intended requirement.

Many reasons contribute to this failure, from the vendor overselling the capability of the system to the team failing to complete detailed design analysis prior to the implementation. Furthermore, many companies are impressed by pretty 3D graphics representing the new system and assume it represents a complete simulation analysis when, in fact, it is nothing but a 3D visualization of the flow.

A very effective method used throughout the industry to avoid design pitfalls is the use of detailed simulation analysis.

Simulation must not be confused with visualization. Visualization is normally a 2D or 3D representation of the flow, showing how equipment interacts and materials flow through the system without putting the system through the rigorous tests of checks and balances that are needed for the system to perform effectively.

Visualization is a great tool to convey concepts, but it differs from simulation analysis, which takes into consideration all of the system constraints. These constraints include downtime, change-over, and spatial layout. Simulation also analyzes system performance in considerable depth.

A detailed simulation analysis should point out weak design areas and potential system interaction problems that are otherwise missed. True system performance, rates, and effect of failures can be analyzed, leaving little room for design errors and surprises during the implementation.

Furthermore, detailed simulation analysis allows designers to put the system through different scenarios and perform what-if analysis and layout analysis. These capabilities allow the team to determine the best system layout before any physical implementation is performed.

In the racking and picking system, proper slotting is required in order to minimize travel and reduce the time to pick and replenish. Slotting is the function of allocating specific items to locations within the warehouse, and is performed based on the velocity of the item, the strike zone, the warehouse congestion impact, and requirements such as brands and item weight.

In any racking system, proper simulation analysis should be performed in order to understand the impact of initial slotting on travel, replenishment, and pick time. Slotting must also be modified after the system is operational and may require constant optimization depending on the variability in the system.

With proper design and upfront analysis, the DC can operate within its proper efficiency requirement. As the system expands, considerations such as equipment downtime, change-over, and variability of shipping and receiving can all start to impact the efficiency.

In situations like this, the team in charge must resist the temptation to simply "fight fires" and should instead focus their energy on conducting proper design changes guided by detailed analysis. A short-term, "fire-fighting" mentality impacts shipment readiness, delays receiving, and hinders automation, resulting in decreased efficiency and increased running costs.

DEFINING THE PROBLEM

This chapter covers the implementation of a warehouse distribution center from receiving to shipping, including all the intricacies discussed above. The goal of the model is to determine answers to the following questions:

- What is the current warehouse picking capacity?
- What is the best picking method for the DC and is there a way to modify our picking to improve efficiency.
- What type of replenishment is required?
- Is there a way to improve receiving in order to minimize time to rack the pallets?
- How can we minimize congestion in staging?
- Is there a better way to slot the warehouse?

The model will be built to answer the above questions. It also needs to be ready to connect to external WMS/WCS in the future in order to provide the shift and plant manager a preview of how the shift will perform.

Note that this preview is a side benefit of an accurate simulation model. Predictive features can be used during day-to-day operation provided that the model can load a valid current state of the warehouse, a good representation of the order being picked, and a list of available resources.

Before going into the main building cycle, it is important to first identify some key components and assumptions for the warehouse:

The data set loaded needs to represent actual SKUs to pick. Each SKU represents an item that can be ordered and is stored at one or more locations within the warehouse.

Each location should have a capacity constraint as to how many items it can store, defined by volume, weight, or count.

Items can be picked as eaches (singles), cartons, or pallets. A carton contains a number of eaches and a pallet contains a number of cartons.

A pick sequence identifying sample orders to be picked. The pick sequence may contain multiple orders per cart and multiple carts/orders per wave.

The above information may be entered into the model or imported from an existing WMS/WCS system.

Item location data is required at this early stage of model-building because the location of each item identifies how efficient the warehouse is. If the locations are changed, the warehouse picking efficiency can improve (or not) depending on the amount of travel required. Therefore, the last piece of information required would be a layout (or initial layout if it is a new warehouse design) to be used for distance calculation.

The following is a sample layout of the warehouse being built:

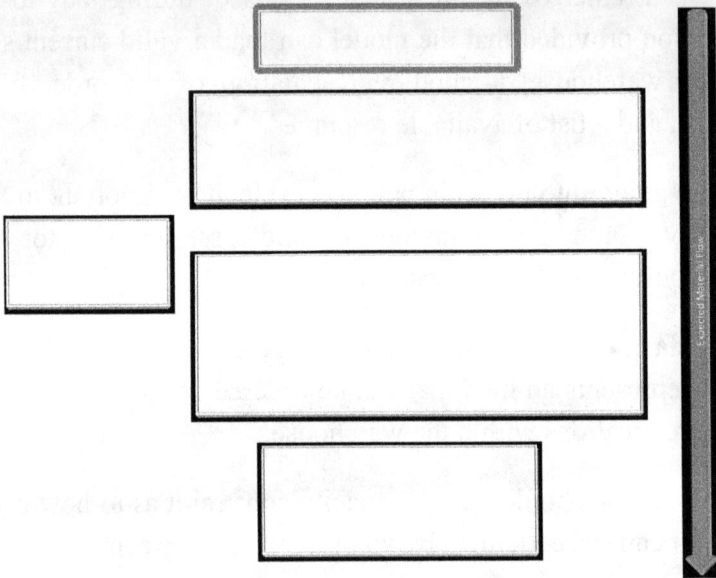

Image 13-1. Sample warehouse layout.

The basic progression of material flow within the warehouse starts at the receiving side. Pallets are received through truck loads, then scanned, quality controlled, and assigned a location in the storage rack area. Pick orders are released from the WMS/WCS system and passed through to the picking assignment area.

After that, each pick sequence is handed off to a picker who travels through the pick front racks in the picking area and collects items into the cart. When the cart is complete, it is dropped off at the staging area for order staging prior to shipping and a new cart sequence starts.

As picking progresses, the number of items in each pick front decreases. These items will need to be replenished once a certain quantity is reached. Replenishment requests are generated, which translate to the transport of a pallet from the storage area to the pick front area to resupply the content of the pick fronts. Of course, failure to properly resupply the pick front will result in order delays as items are not available to be picked.

The above over-simplification of the warehouse operation is key to creating a valid model at the end. Since all warehouses share the same core model with some variation, having a solid base will help in future phases to expand the operation.

DATA COLLECTION

Now that problem and first phase are defined, the next step will be to collect the initial data set.

First, identify the dimensions of the warehouse. In the case of an existing warehouse, load the CAD drawing to be used for distance calculation. In the case of a new warehouse, load a sample dimension set that will help in laying out the warehouse flow.

Next, identify the naming convention for the racks. Naming is a critical component of the build process as each SKU will be stored in a specific location identified by the WMS. Therefore in order to minimize confusion between the imported data set and model, it is best to use the same naming convention used in the WMS. Note that this does not limit the type of items stored at a location; it only identifies the location names.

If the rack sizes are known, collect the dimensions of the existing racking system and any potential storage constraint such as weight limit, height constraints, and others.

Generate a sample SKU to location map. In existing warehouses, the data must exist in the WMS system, while in new green field type implementations, a random assignment or best guess works at this stage.

Identify the time it takes to pick an item from the rack, potential travel speed of the picker, and travel speed of any MHE equipment being used (for example, fork trucks).

Set up potential pick sequences based on order profile. In existing warehouses, the data is readily available in the WMS and it consists of the actual picking method used at the warehouse. In green field type implementations, a data creation module can be used to mimic the potential new warehouse being analyzed.

PHASE 1: CONSTRUCTION OF BASIC MODEL

The first phase of the model implementation consists of creating the pick front area. This area, in any warehouse, contains the bulk of the operation and the majority of the material movement required.

The model consists of an initial pick sequence generator or sequencer that will generate cart requests to be loaded. Each cart contains a number of SKUs to be picked. After the cart is generated, it is passed to the pre-pick process, which in this phase consists of a single process with a set amount of time.

Similarly, at the end of the flow, a process is set up to stage all picked carts and pass them to the loading area, which in this case marks the end of the model.

In order to complete the picks, the actual racks need to be implemented based on a set naming convention. Each rack consists of multiple bays and levels, each with a unique identifier as defined in the WMS. The time required to implement the racking system is dependent on the simulation tool being used and method of racking implementation.

For example, using a single process representation for a 20 bay rack is not as detailed as implementing all 20 bays. This in turn is less detailed than creating each level in each bay, which would generate some 100 different locations assuming a five-level racking system. Some simulation tools contain specific building blocks that simplify the implementation and naming of the racks. These reduce the amount of time required to build the rack definition.

In the case of the example in this chapter, the team used Simcad Process Simulator to implement the racks, which included both a rack-building module and complete rack builder based on a Microsoft Excel® input file. By loading the rack definition into the module, the simulator creates the complete racking system with a single click. Through the use of this technology, such a time consuming task was completed in a matter of minutes instead of the weeks it would have taken with other tools.

After the racks are built, the model needs to define the pick path for the pickers. Connecting the racks in directional pick paths identifies the aisles that a picker can go through, and by defining them based on modules, it is easy to make changes to the path in the future. In addition, congestion control can be implemented by allowing only a certain number of pickers in a specific area. This control will be added later on in the modeling process.

After picking is complete, a sample staging area is created using a set of conveyor belts and multiple docking stations. The staging area is for representation only at this point and will be expanded to its full detail as the model is developed in future phases.

The following is a representation of the completed model:

Image 13-2. 2D and 3D representation of the generated model. Also shown is the pick path and aisle travel of the pickers.

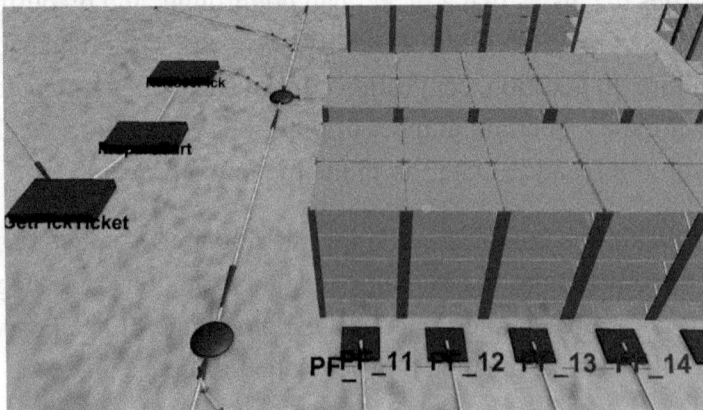

Image 13-3. Detailed view of the pre-pick area.

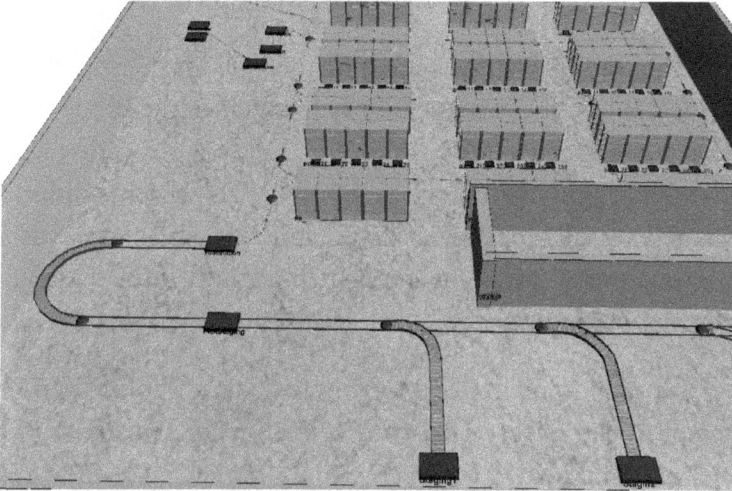

Image 13-4. Model with staging area.

The next step in this phase is to load the data set into the model. Each SKU to be picked is identified with a location (while maintaining that a location can contain multiple SKUs). A sample pick sequence is also loaded to be used in the validation stage.

PHASE 1A: VALIDATION

The model is now ready for initial validation before entering the analysis and optimization phase. The following points need to be addressed:

- Does the picker follow the required pick path identified in the data set?
- Do we have all of the pick front racks implemented and named correctly?
- What are the metrics for the model and how do they compare to the actual environment?

In order to test out the pick path concept, create a single pick sequence and identify one SKU per rack to pick.

For each of the SKUs, 1) check the model and make sure that the rack location is in the model, 2) is mapped to the proper SKU, and 3) has enough quantity for testing. One simplification here is to avoid managing inventory at this stage and assume unlimited inventory at all locations. This strategy will serve as an approximation at this point since the model does not yet have its replenishment logic set up.

With the sample pick sequence implemented, run the model at slow speed and observe the path of the picker. This path, if the model is implemented correctly, should traverse the flow based on the defined sequence and picks an item from each of the locations defined.

Before moving further into the validation cycle, the picker logic needs to be fully validated. Correct any issues with the picker progress, then add a pick time to each of the items in order to validate the total time required to pick. By assigning a constant pick time, the modeler can quickly compute the total pick time required and compare it to the model output.

Note that this decision assumes that the simulation tool animation is a representation of the simulation engine progress. If that is not the case in the tool used, additional offline analysis needs to be performed and the validation time will extend to a few days instead of a few minutes.

With the picker logic validated, the next step is to validate that all pick front locations are implemented and named correctly. To perform this validation step, create a pick sequence that picks each SKU in the system and from all potential pick front locations.

Be careful to ensure that all pick front locations are picked from. Do not simply rely on the SKU sequence, as there could be a situation where not all pick front have SKUs assigned to them. In that case, a dummy SKU can be used for validation and entered into the data set. Since the temporary SKUs will never be picked from the WMS, they will not impact the future model in case the modeler does not remove them from the data set.

With the pick sequence defined, the modeler should run the simulation and identify any locations that are missing within the flow. The simulation tool should be able to generate a report identifying the missing locations, if any, so that they can be added. At this point, a spaghetti diagram should be run and analyzed as it will generate a perfect representation of pick path and all locations that are picked from.

Now that the modeler has completed the two key validation steps, it is important to validate the pre-pick area and make sure the proper timing and constraints are correct. Additional validation of the pick sequence can be made at this point. To test out multiple carts per pick sequence, multiple orders per cart, the wave sequencing, etc. Again through predetermined and predefined pick sequences.

Note that all the validation steps need to be made based on predefined, known, and simplified pick sequences in order to identify logic errors within the model. The goal is to validate the model at this point; analysis comes after.

By now, the model has all the required components to run an actual pick sequence, generated either by the WMS or by a data generation tool that will create a mock-up pick sequence based on the warehouse constraints. The modeler needs to identify a previous day of operation and pull the pick sequences along with the computed metrics (Lines/minute, units/minute, orders/minute, and so on).

In addition, the modeler needs to break the lead time calculation of each pick sequence to identify the travel time in the aisles, travel time to rack from cart, time to pick the items, and the associated travel distances. Although the WMS or existing metrics system may not have those metrics computed, any additional information that can be used to point out potential irregularities within the model should be computed.

With the generated data compared to existing metrics (based on availability), the model is now ready for analysis.

One item to note is that, at this point, no actual picker constraint has been added. Therefore the model needs to limit the number of carts in the picking area to the number of pickers available to pick. The resource constraint will be added at a later phase.

PHASE 1B: ANALYSIS

At this point the model is considered data driven with built-in constraints. As the modeler changes the input data set of where the SKU is located, the pick sequences configuration, the wave configuration, pick time per item, and so on, the model will generate the corresponding metrics associated with the loaded data. The constraints on the warehouse itself do not change, but the loaded data set does.

One of the goals of the simulation is to determine the capacity of the pick front area: how many items can be picked per minute?

As with the previous models, the goal is to compute a theoretical maximum which identifies the maximum throughput possible and assumes there are no operational constraints on the system.

Either the WMS generated data set, a new data set, or a hybrid of both can now be run on the model in order to push more picks through it. While watching the lead time for the carts and the number of items picked (from the displayed metrics), the modeler needs to keep expanding the data set until the number of items per minute flattens out.

In fact, due to the congestion factor, pushing too many pick carts into the pick front area will, at some point, increase the lead time and reduce the pick rate of the warehouse. The solution is not to increase the number of pick carts, but to organize the warehouse to minimize the number of pick carts (and pickers) while generating the lowest lead time and maximum throughput.

If a scenario analyzer is integrated with the simulation tool (as is the case with the tool used in this example, Simcad Process Simulator), all generated data from the runs is compiled and analyzed in the scenario analyzer. Otherwise, the data needs to be tabulated and exported out to external tools for analysis.

The final analysis of this phase should provide the maximum number of carts needed and the maximum lines/minute that can be achieved from the pick area. This number is our theoretical maximum. Any capacity requirement beyond those numbers requires a pick front expansion, complete re-slotting of the pick fronts, or a combination of both.

The second phase of the implementation is to add resource constraints and full replenishment to the pick fronts. It is also beneficial at this stage to load a set of work standards to be applied to the model runtime.

To implement the resources, the modeler needs to identify the type of resources available, the order generator/controller, the picker, the replenisher, and any other potential resources required for the pick front implementation. The resource is then applied to individual process steps to implement the proper constraints.

Additionally, resources need to be applied to travel paths. Especially the pickers and replenishers, as the pick and replenishment paths need to be traveled by both resources with or without a pallet or cart.

Both resources need to remain within their cart/pallet until the sequence is complete, then grab a different one. The resource cannot, in this case, drop a cart in the middle of a pick sequence for another resource to pick it up. This behavior is not common in a warehouse and should not be in the model, unless a zone pick implementation is used which requires resource allocation per zone and not per cart.

The next step is to enable the replenishment process. Each pick location should decrease its count every time an item is picked. When the quantity, at the locations, drops below the replenishment threshold count, a request for replenishment is made and a pallet is picked from storage and unloaded at the appropriate location. If the location cannot hold a full pallet, the location is replenished and the pallet is returned to storage.

Otherwise the full pallet is unloaded and the empty pallet is returned to empty storage.

When a pallet request is made, the pallet needs to wait at the pickup location until a replenishment resource is available to perform the move. The replenishment resource needs to pick up a full (or partial) pallet and move it to the pick front location for replenishment. At the pick front location, the pallet needs to be opened and unloaded so that it is ready for picking.

During that process, and if replenishment occurs on the same side of picking, the picking cycle will be delayed. After location replenishment is complete, the empty pallet needs to be moved to an empty collection location before a new location can be replenished. In the case where partial pallets are allowed after replenishment, the partial pallet will need to be returned to the storage area.

Both picking and replenishment should be based on the type of item being processed and the location of that item. Depending on the item weight, grab factor, location height, and other such factors, the cycle varies throughout the warehouse. It is therefore best to identify a standard for picking based on all the factors.

An example is a time to pick a single item from the strike zone (most efficient way to pick), along with a variation based on weight, volume, and location height. By implementing the timing properties in this form, the slotting representation of the warehouse will start to impact the overall efficiency and pick rate.

The model, after it's validated, represents a complete warehouse including:

- SKU level inventory control,

- Rack analysis and percent rack occupancy,
- Pick path distance calculation and optimization,
- Replenishment sequences and flow, and
- Most importantly, congesting analysis and avoidance.

Hence, at this point of the warehouse modeling project, the developed simulation model can be used for daily analysis of the warehouse and as a tool to visualize and analyze the shift progress in the picking area before it starts. Having a good insight on the issues that may occur during the day creates a proactive management and problem avoidance environment that greatly increases the efficiency of the warehouse.

PHASE 2A: VALIDATION

To validate the model, the modeler first needs to ensure that the original Phase 1 model is still intact. Since Phase 1 has already produced the required data to test, the same data set needs to be used in all the validation phases. For Phase 2, the team needs to validate the resource application on picking and replenishment, the replenishment process, and the time factor application.

First, the replenishment process needs to be validated in order to make sure the flow is correct and proper inventory tracking is controlled. Using the first pick sequence data set with simplified model, the modeler needs to modify the replenishment rate to be one item below the current loaded quantity. This means that a replenishment request is made as soon as an item is picked. Next, the modeler runs the sequence through and observes the replenishment requests.

For each request, a pallet needs to be picked up from storage and delivered to the correct pick front, items unloaded and inventory quantity updated, and the empty pallet returned to the empty pallet storage area. Only after the team has ensured that the resources are properly applied can a full validation of the warehouse be accomplished.

As the sample data set is run, the model can also be observed for resource allocation. The picker needs to stay with the cart for the duration of the pick sequence and move items from the rack to the cart. When the sequence is complete, the picker needs to walk back to the new order station and start a new cart.

The same applies to the replenisher, which needs to stay with the pallet until the replenishment process is complete, then walk back to pick another pallet. As a secondary validation, the modeler should add a resource count for both pickers and replenishers. The model should only allow the proper number into the flow.

Having finished validating the resources, the next step is to validate the complete model. The data set loaded should be the pick sequence that passes through each location. By setting the replenishment level to "1" under the current quantity, all pick fronts should undergo a picking and replenishing sequence based on the order (or cart) picking sequence.

The last portion of Phase 2A Validation involves **validating the pick and travel time**. Following the same concept as the previous validation set, the model needs to be checked to make sure the timing properties are based on the location being picked from and the distance of travel.

Image 13-5. Completed model showing travel path.

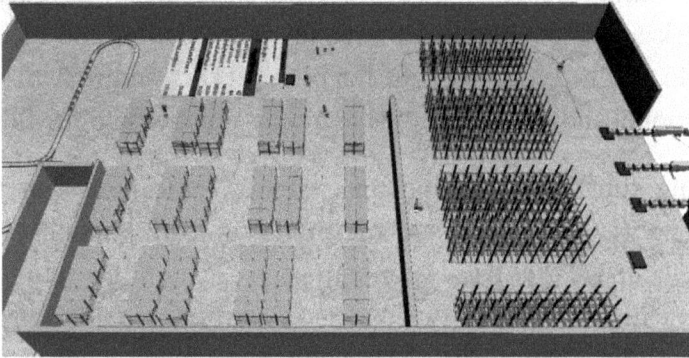

Image 13-6. Completed model – no travel path.

Picking Results	
Picker Utilization =	90.39
Pick Seq/Hr =	60.00
PickEfficiency	
Total Lines =	1200
Total Units =	2354
LinesPerHour =	170.62
UnitsPerHour =	334.69
Lines/LaborHour =	42.66
Units/LaborHour =	83.67
Statistics	
Lines/LeadTime =	59.00
Units/Leadtime =	116.00

Image 13-7. Sample model metrics.

PHASE 2B: ANALYSIS AND OPTIMIZATION

The analysis phase starts by loading actual data into the model. Each SKU should be allocated to a pick front location. The quantity for each should be set as well. The model initially assumes unlimited storage, when a replenishment is called for, a random storage location is used to retrieve the proper pallet. This setting eliminates the need to load the slotting of the storage area if it is not available and the need to expand the receiving/staging area.

The pick sequences also need to be loaded for a specific duration. If the model is used for short term analysis, a single shift pick sequence can be loaded. If a longer term analysis is required, then the model needs to include an extended set of pick sequences that spans days or months. In either case, the data can remain in the WMS data set and be retrieved on demand when needed (provided that the tool allows for live data connectivity during the model run).

The resulting analysis should provide the following:

Lead time per pick sequence, including a breakdown for aisle travel, cart to rack travel, pick time, congestion wait time, and additional time for all non-picking related activities

The number of items per sequence, orders per sequence, carts per sequence (if applicable), and delay time due to replenishment in the picking process

Lead time per replenishment, including a breakdown for aisle travel, pallet load and unload, travel time outside the aisle, and congestion delay (waiting for pick or other replenishment to complete)

As a final analysis piece, the model should generate a spaghetti diagram of the picking area for picking and replenishment (with separate views), along with a picking heat map identifying the heavily used racks (high velocity) within the warehouse.

A final summary is a combined report that shows the picking/replenishment wait time as it relates to the heat map and spaghetti diagram. Just because a rack location is accessed more than others does not mean that congestion is a problem next to that location. The model provides a correlation between the heat map/spaghetti diagram and overall system congestion. This correlation is the true measure used to identify if slotting is a problem in the warehouse and potential areas to improve from an optimization point of view.

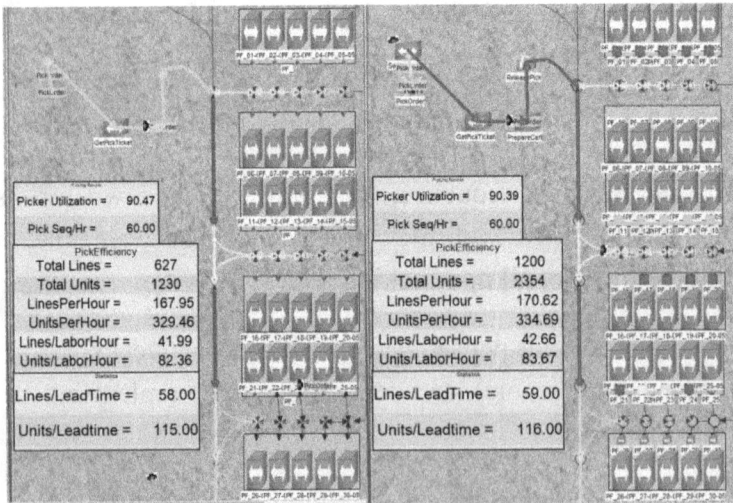

Image 13-8. Spaghetti diagram and heat map with congestion.

PHASE 3: INCREASE DETAILS

The last phase of the warehouse implementation is to expand storage, receiving, and the outbound staging and truck loading areas.

The storage implementation is very similar to the pick front area except that it is storing pallets instead of eaches or cases. Therefore, to expand storage, the modeler follows the same modeling concepts used in picking.

Inbound receiving needs to be expanded based on a truck arrival schedule, the unload sequence, and pallet transfer to storage. The truck arrival schedule is normally provided based on date/time and SKUs received. If the schedule is not available, a good distribution of arrival for each truck and its content will be sufficient.

Note that if the distribution is off and a certain SKU quantity is depleted from storage, then picking and replenishment is affected.

As pallets are received, some mixed pallets may need to be opened, sorted, and re-palletized before they go into storage. If this scenario exists, then the model needs to expand the receiving area and include resource constraints for all process steps. Incorrect implementation in this area generates invalid results at the end of the run.

After the pallets are ready, they need to be moved to a storage location based on SKU. This is normally part of the storage process and is similar to replenishment in picking with the exception that the pallets are stored as a unit instead of expanding them into eaches or cartons.

Outbound staging and shipping is slightly more complex than inbound because carts need to be grouped by orders, orders grouped by delivery, and deliveries organized by truck routes. In many cases, outbound staging is developed as a separate model and then imported into the main warehouse model. The availability of model connectivity and model import is an important feature that allows multiple modelers to work on different sections of the model, then combine them into a single cohesive model.

PHASE 3A: VALIDATION

The validation for Phase 3 is very similar to Phase 2 progression. The same test sequence should be performed to make sure all storage locations are properly labeled and implemented and that all received pallets are stored at their appropriate destination. Storage resources need to be checked in order to limit the number of pallets being stored or reconfigured in the mixed pallet area.

From this point, the model can be expanded and fine-tuned to support the intricacies of the warehouse. Depending on the warehouse culture and whether management is ready for predictive analytics, the model can be used for daily analysis of warehouse activities prior to a shift start and as a comparison after the shift completes.

RE-SLOTTING THE WAREHOUSE

Throughout this chapter, a number of references were made to slotting the warehouse and slotting's impact on warehouse efficiency. Unfortunately, slotting the warehouse based on SKU velocity, rack strike zone, brands, types, and weights is never the most efficient slotting method.

Efficient slotting is only achieved when pick sequences and congestion factors are applied and added to the slotting computation equation. Combining multiple high-velocity items in a single aisle or multiple adjacent racks creates unnecessary congestion that delays the overall picking cycle and reduces the efficiency of the warehouse. Additionally, seasonality and pick orders sequence have an impact on which slotting method should be used and which item locations should be selected.

Slotting in a warehouse should be determined by multiple analysis steps, starting with traditional slotting implementation based on velocity, strike zone, item weight, pick preference and recursive or repeating congestion factor. Consideration of the congestion factor is driven by the warehouse operation.

The only way to identify congestion correctly is to analyze the current picking methods against the existing warehouse slotting. Keep in mind that re-slotting the warehouse comes at a cost; moving items from one location to another requires resources and time, and added congestion and delay can occur during the move.

An efficient slotting method factors in the future pick sequences based on forecasted constraints, then identifies the value of each SKU re-slot. If the cost of moving the SKUs is higher than the increased cost of keeping them at their current location, then re-slotting for that SKU is beneficial. Otherwise, it is a waste of money and resources.

Simulation software can perform more detailed slotting analysis provided that the software has no limit on the amount of data loaded and can process the warehouse based on individual locations and SKUs. If data limits exist in the simulation tool, then the generated slotting is based on a distribution, which renders the results highly ineffective and defeats the purpose of the slotting optimization.

RECAP

As this chapter has discussed, the complexity of any warehousing endeavor should not be underestimated. There are many elements of a distribution center that must be incorporated into a model, and only after these attributes have all been considered can the model truly represent the reality of day-to-day operations.

With the proper technology, even a highly variable environment can be simulated, understood, and predicted. The following chapter discusses dynamic simulation technology in greater detail.

Chapter 14: Dynamic Simulation Technology

The uses of simulation vary widely, spanning many different industries and accomplishing many tasks within those industries. Understandably, these many functions require powerful technology.

Although processor speeds have increased rapidly in recent years, simulation, due to its extensive computational and visualization requirements, has consistently challenged and used the processors to their full power. With evolving 64-bit simulation engine technology, simulation models have increased in size and complexity with larger memory requirements, ever-expanded data input sets, and increased connectivity requirements.

In addition, real-time data is becoming more accessible than ever, and it has greatly contributed to the accuracy, validity, and usability of simulation models.

The increased demand for powerful simulation software is good news, but it is important that the software's capabilities match the customer's needs. This chapter discusses simulation technology in more depth and describes how real-time predictive and prescriptive analytics powered by simulation and real-time data connectivity can harness the power of simulation to its fullest potential.

INTRODUCTION

In every industry, from manufacturing to services to logistics to healthcare, there is an increasing need to do more with less, increase efficiency while reducing cost, and improve utilization while maximizing throughput. Process improvement is a constant, never-ending effort that strives to achieve better performance with current or reduced resources. As improvement in one area is achieved, other opportunities arise and new ideas are tested and implemented.

Simulation is a valuable tool that many organizations have taken advantage of. It allows a risk-free environment to manipulate conditions and examine the outcomes of different changes. It also provides a more complete understanding of the process flow and helps to explain the intricacies of an operation to stakeholders.

As simulation models span larger and larger operations—full warehouses, manufacturing plants, hospital campuses, and so on—the models become more complex. They grow computationally invasive and require more time to run using traditional, single-threaded simulation environments.

Take for example a warehousing implementation. This hypothetical warehouse involves multiple ASRS systems, standard racking, AGVs for material handling, automation equipment, high speed lines, and, most importantly, human workers consistently interacting with all aspects of the warehouse.

To drive such a system, data must be available from the WMS, WCS, PLCs, RFID, and other data points tracked through systems such as ERP, SAP, barcode, RTLS, GPS, or manual entry.

For offline runs, waiting for the model to complete the run is not as critical or demanding. On the other hand, when the model is providing real-time predictive analytics, model run turn-around time, including multiple scenarios and Monte Carlo runs, becomes critical.

Whether the implementation is for schedule adherence, predictive bottleneck detection, efficiency monitoring and improvement, or maintenance and bottleneck alerts, two key factors impact the overall solution: simulation speed, and model validity and accuracy.

Simulation speeds can be improved by better utilizing the underlying hardware system. Still, whether the team uses smaller, independent and interacting models or a highly-distributed single model implementation, challenges can arise in model synchronization and real-time data availability. As discussed later, there are many methods that can be implemented to successfully distribute the model and achieve extensive improvement in simulation run speed without disturbing model validity.

Model accuracy, on the other hand, can be more difficult to achieve, especially when real-time data is used. In the case of static environments, the modeler is aware of the different process steps and paths that parts or resources take. Model constraints can be imposed using the known data and current constraints.

In the case of real-time data and real-time predictive environments, models need to be designed in a way that allows them to grow with the system, enable real-time constraint changes, and in some cases, expand themselves in order to maintain the correct relationship with live data.

In other words, models must run within an intelligent environment that allows them to modify their constraints or process steps based on data feedback from external data sources and without human intervention. This is a key requirement that enables systems to be used as turn-key, hands-off systems that are constantly evolving within their environment while maintaining a high degree of validity and accuracy.

CHALLENGES

Questions often arise in meetings, offline discussions, and in the minds of designers: how many hospital beds do we need? Is our warehouse slotting optimized? How much buffering do we need to support a manual operation? How can we better schedule our tanks? What is the impact of the cleaning cycle?

The list goes on, and it can vary by industry, but the main question is this: how do we allocate our resources to optimize efficiency?

In the case of simple systems, where a single input, a single output and a constant feed rate produce a single product, computing the system throughput and OEE is simple. Unfortunately, a closed loop system with a single product type is seldom the case.

Automated systems are built to handle multiple product types and variations in order to meet their ROI. To complicate things further, different products require different speed rates, change-over, and sometimes labor requirements. All of these constraints contribute to the overall system throughput and OEE, making a simple formula computation an invalid and inaccurate representation.

A common mistake in throughput calculation occurs when operations promise customer deliveries based on the high OEE of individual components. Although each independent sub-component performs at the designed specifications, the overall system OEE is lower due to component interactions, product variations and other unexpected delays. Equipment ROI is not achieved, order delays become a common occurrence, and frustration sets in.

These complex circumstances require complex simulations in order to determine answers to the questions at hand. Using intelligent simulation environments comes with its own set of challenges.

When simulation models interact, they need to be intelligently synchronized in order to protect the integrity of the results and validity of the model. Whether the implementation spans a single system using multi-threading methods or multiple systems using inter-processor synchronization, the synchronization itself is a key item that must be controlled.

In addition to the synchronization challenge, simulations interacting with external, real-time data systems must maintain the integrity of that integration with outside systems. In other words, real-time data needs to be clearly mapped to the model in a way that prevents ambiguity while providing an efficient redundancy level.

Whether the data is being retrieved from external data stores (such as databases, SAP, WMS, ERP, or EMR, among others) or received asynchronously through PLCs or RFID data, the simulation model(s) automatically update and the outcomes of the changing conditions are used to identify bottlenecks and areas for improvement in real-time.

The most valuable aspect of intelligent models is their ability to constantly evolve based on the real-time environment without disturbing the validity of the model. Such models are designed to adapt to incoming data and add or remove constraints based on the actual environment. Intelligent models constantly learn from the current environment, readjust on-the-fly, and consistently perform validation, analysis, and optimization in order to create a hands-free simulation environment.

MODEL-BUILDING

An interconnected network of simulation models can exist in three forms:

1. Model output(s) feeding one or many model inputs,
2. Tightly synchronized models in a multi-threading environment, or
3. Distributed processing with synchronized models across the overall system.

When real-time data connectivity is used, the methodology is not as critical as the modeling approach. In cases using real-time data and controls such as RFID, GPS, and other RTLS time systems, simulation models should be built and defined to allow for the external tracking system to automatically update and modify the model behavior and constraints.

For example, if a fork truck item is transitioning to a new pallet location, the model should be smart enough to allow the movement and automatically update the model constraints with the new location.

Each model can be used in multiple ways:

- Real-time visibility showing the location of each item, progress and analytics for every entity within the system

- Predictive mode where the model constantly runs in the background, consuming historical data, processing real-time constraints, and generating predictive analytics while providing alerts and notifications as to the impact on the future state of the operation
- Prescriptive mode where the model optimizes the future state and processes changes required to improve the efficiency of the operations' predicted future state

Whether rescheduling jobs, labor, or deliveries, re-sequencing the line with updated WCS or PLC logic, or modifying process flow and processing constraints, a prescriptive mode provides for an optimized future state with minimal human interaction and no offline analysis required.

AN INTELLIGENT MODEL WITH REAL-TIME CONNECTIVITY

Whether connected to an HL7 data feed, WMS, WCS, ERP, or RTLS system, each model needs to be able to modify itself in order to support the data feed. Self-modifying models are able to detect changes in the external environment and constantly evolve in order to support the new constraints.

Some examples of the capabilities of an evolving model would be adding new rooms to an emergency department, changing the pick path in a warehouse, adding a new rack, inserting a new machine into the flow, or generating a new assembly type.

Self-evolving simulation models are built in a dynamic environment where models can be updated and modified during the simulation run. This is an inherent capability of the simulation tool being used; otherwise the models are static and require constant human intervention.

In addition, the simulation tool needs to allow the internal model distributions to be auto-recomputed based on historical data as well as new data generated from real-time systems or other simulation models. This feature is required in order for the underlying simulation engine to drive the Monte Carlo analysis. This is incorporated in both predictive and prescriptive environments.

As with the interactive environment, dynamic simulators have an integrated ability to connect to data systems at runtime, and they have a feature that allows them to retrieve data from external data sources instead of storing it locally. This feature often reduces the local footprint of the model and enables the execution of larger data sets.

For a predictive environment to be valid, the simulation model needs to have the ability to load an accurate representation of the current state of the operation. The initial state can be made available through tracking systems, ERP/EMR or similar systems, or other operation control systems that contain a representation of one or more areas of the operation.

Note that the data set representing the current state may be fragmented across multiple systems, which should be combined in order to provide a true representation. The environment used must allow for multiple data connectivity and data manipulation in order to create the needed relationship between the different data sets.

For example, a tracking system may provide information on the location of providers or MHE devices, while an EMR or ERP system provides the type of action taken. By combining the two systems, the environment should be smart enough to connect the presence of the person to the actions taken based on flow progress.

The initial state is necessary because the simulation model must start with the known, real-world environment before it predicts the future of the operation. Every time a new set of analysis is generated, a new initial state is loaded into the prediction and simulation model in order to provide the most accurate predictive environment. The more knowledge the model has of the current state, the more accurate the prediction engine will be.

Two key advantages are apparent in the use of a dynamic simulator:

There is no limit to the amount of data or number of data sources that can be available to the simulator. In other words, since the system can connect to existing ERP, MRP, WCS, and WMS systems, as well as pull in the current state, previous behavior, and future orders, it can perform a simulation analysis without requiring any model changes.

The developed model can also be used for daily scheduling and analysis activities. Since the model is already developed and connected to actual systems, a daily run can provide insight on the daily outlook and allow managers to be better prepared to handle any potential problems that may arise. These models can be run in a non-automated (manual) mode and provide the required predictions as needed. For example, a warehouse manager can run the next shift on the simulator and identify the required manpower, efficiency, delays, replenishment requirements, and completion time for all orders in the shift.

By utilizing the built features of a dynamic simulator, all required analysis values can be generated from the model and saved for either custom reporting or web-enabled dashboard views. Lead times, utilization, efficiency, throughput rates and cycle times are all integral parts of the model and can be displayed or analyzed as part of the model view.

The generated analysis data set should be stored for historical analysis and eventual comparison with standards and the current operation. This data can later be analyzed in order to produce different standards for each operation within the system. Care must be taken to ensure that the data is coherent and does not overlap; otherwise, it will be nearly impossible to use it in the predictive engine for future runs.

The animated environment of a dynamic simulator is highly effective for visualization purposes. The animation can actually represent the current state of the operation if the model runs in real time, including a demonstration of how current constraints impact the system behavior and analytics.

Running a model offline with initial state loading or connectivity to the internal data component will generate a true animated representation of the flow that can be viewed from any location.

The generated animation representing the current state of the model can be viewed in multiple formats, including 2D animation, 3D animation, virtual reality mode, VSMs, and more. The representation depends on the tool capability as long as the true data connectivity is made available.

The data generated by the live model can now be displayed in different formats, from overall performance metrics to section-specific information. In addition, the system can display current deviation from standards, a dynamic value stream based on current numbers, and other metrics required to manage the operation effectively.

Because all systems evolve over time, the model constantly needs to adapt to any changes in the actual environment. By using the capabilities of dynamic simulators, the model can evolve as live systems change. When new locations are added, a new machine is defined, or an extra AGV is inserted in the system, the model dynamically changes behavior and applies the necessary alterations to the model with minimal human interaction.

As the system evolves and models interact, metrics are dynamically generated and can be used for tracking, visibility, predictive analytics, and prescriptive analytics.

PREDICTIVE ANALYTICS

An intelligent, dynamic simulation model has the ability to learn from the current environment and evolve itself in order to improve its predictive values.

The model begins based on the initial constraints defined within its settings. This is considered the system startup and occurs once per model per installation. This startup run serves two main purposes: 1) generating the initial current model state, and 2) collecting external constraints that influence the model progress, including downtime, cycle times, arrival patterns and others.

As the predictive model evolves, the following operations occur:

General distributions of cycle times, arrival patterns, downtime, and other factors are computed at each run. Historical distributions are computed based on change factors and patterns that relate to the validity of the data. For example, data points from the operation's far history are weighed less than near history, and current daily events have more impact than either of the historical data sets. Known data sets containing near-future schedule or shipping requirements also impact the generated analytics.

Multiple Monte Carlo runs are performed in order to avoid the variability created from the distribution and to establish a valid and accurate representation of the future of the operation.

Data generated from the predictive model is displayed directly to web-enabled dashboards, providing insight into the current and future status of the operation. The predictive environment generated is highly accurate because it is derived from real-time constraints driven by a distribution of current, historical and known future data sets.

Real-time schedule adherence is generated based on the current status and predicted future of each operation. Schedule deviation, slippage, and on-time deliveries are dynamically computed and displayed to the user. Alerts are generated when unexpected events occur or schedule slippage is detected. The predictive model is able to determine the number of generated delays, their cause, and their potential impact on other sections of the operation.

PRESCRIPTIVE ANALYTICS

In the prescriptive model mode, real-time optimization and validation are performed in the background. Much like in the predictive environment, Monte Carlo runs are taken in order to determine the viability of each potential optimization method. The number of required runs is determined by the system and is driven by model convergence factors as they relate to the optimized values.

Examples of real-time optimization include identifying the best pick route and pick schedule for a warehouse, modifying put-away and replenishment sequences, altering schedules, man-power requirements or maintenance schedules in a manufacturing environment, or re-scheduling operating room patients based on OR load levels, delays, and current state impact.

During the real-time optimization, a number of potential improvements can be determined. Each viable solution requires a number of changes to the real system in order for the predicted results to be valid. The system can react to the optimization suggestion in different ways depending on its configuration.

The simulation environment provides a unique feature that tests out all of the potential optimization methods and compares them. In addition, advantages and disadvantages of each option can be provided to the team in order to simplify the decision-making process.

The team should accept the requested change if it fits within the "allowed" change constraints, then propagate the change to the external system and proceed with tracking.

The system should present the user with a number of options and allow the decision to be made by the manager in charge. When a solution is accepted, the system can either push the change to external systems or monitor the environment for change. In this case, it is the manager's responsibility to effect the change on the external system.

Another key benefit of prescriptive analytics is its impact on schedule adherence. As different optimization options are selected, the system presents insights into the future of on-time delivery along with potential impact of change from the current state.

In other words, each optimization method impacts the on-time delivery and efficiency of the environment. Those changes, delays or improvements are posted on live dashboards with varying degrees of detail depending on the dashboard audience.

MULTIPLE COLLABORATION MODELS

For the system to be effective, the implementation should be divided into multiple interconnected models working together to provide the final results. The models can run in three different modes:

Synchronized mode, where multiple models are synchronized in time, constraints and behavior in order to provide a faster execution state in a more controlled environment. There is no limit to the number of synchronized models that can be run, and multiple hardware platforms may be used in order to speed up the execution.

Sequential mode, where multiple models build on each other's results. When the first model completes, it creates the input data set for the next model to run. Upon model start, the second model reloads its constraints, auto-computes its distribution, and proceeds with the execution.

Note that in a sequential mode, a model run may consist of multiple Monte Carlo runs working together to generate the input to the next model.

The third mode is a **hybrid implementation of sequential and synchronized modes**. Based on the system requirements and result definition, the model execution can switch from synchronized to sequential multiple times during the execution cycle.

In all modes, the underlying scheduler in SimTrack takes care of all required synchronization and sequential execution as defined in the system properties.

The burden of synchronizing the model is now a standard functionality of the controlling system, which reduces the requirement on the model developer to implement more stringent synchronization methods. The resulting environment is scalable in execution speed, model complexity and overall system accuracy.

SUMMARY

The presented environment is designed to provide a complete predictive and prescriptive environment built on dynamic, real-time changing, simulation models. *SimTrack, a CreateASoft product*, takes the simulation environment to the next level and makes it an integral part of any organization toolset. The generated data set, whether in real-time visibility or the predictive or prescriptive environment, enables organizations to take advantage of the power of simulation to maximize operational effectiveness and improve on-time delivery and scheduling.

Existing systems implemented in healthcare, manufacturing, and warehousing have proven to be indispensable and have generated an ROI that far exceeds the initial implementation cost within the first year.

Dynamic simulators provide the proper tools and analytics required to analyze and troubleshoot today's complex systems. As new constraints are identified, designers change their dynamic models and use the interactive reporting and visualization in order to define and validate new solutions.

With data connectivity and tracking systems becoming the norm, dynamic simulators are finding their way into the daily routine of designers, managers, operators, and process improvement specialists. Due to their design openness, dynamic simulators can interact with tracking systems (RFID, barcode, GPS, etc.) and machine PLCs to create a visual picture of the present, accurately replay past events for analysis, and forecast the future of the operation.

Dynamic simulators, coupled with integrated dashboards and alerts, provide a rich and more complete environment that rivals the analysis and forecasting of current MES systems on the market today. Moreover, the ROI of dynamic simulators far exceeds their implementation cost as they provide optimization of the current state while forging an efficient analysis path for all future changes to the operation.

RECAP

This book has aimed to outline the countless benefits of simulation technology to the efficiency of any business. While simulation modeling can seem like a daunting task, the use of powerful, interactive simulation technology can simplify these efforts so that the team can spend less time creating the simulation and more time putting it to good use.

Those uses are as broad as the operations themselves. They can vary from answering questions about surgical carts in hospitals to scheduling employees and resources in a distribution center.

With the right tools, managers in any industry can better understand their operations and optimize their process flow and resources. In short, powerful technology helps any manager to find success in simulation.

Appendix A

SIMULATION TECHNOLOGIES USED

SIMCAD PROCESS SIMULATOR

Simcad Process Simulator is an on-the-fly, interactive simulation software that supports discrete and continuous simulation modeling, optimization and analysis. Simcad Process Simulator is developed and distributed by CreateASoft, Inc (https://www.createasoft.com) of Aurora, IL.

Simcad Process Simulator was originally released in February 1996. This book uses Simcad Pro Elite version 13.1 for manufacturing and warehousing implementation. Simcad Pro Health version 13.1, a variant dedicated to the healthcare industry, is used to develop the healthcare simulation models.

SIMTRACK – TRACKING, PREDICTIVE, AND PRESCRIPTIVE ANALYTICS

SimTrack transitions the simulation technology to a real-time, predictive and prescriptive environment. SimTrack connects to multiple data systems and technologies such as RTLS, Bar Code, GPS, PLC, EMR, WMS, WCS, SAP, ERP, and others, in order to provide a complete view of the operation. The automatically collected data is used for tracking visualization, operation optimization and control, predictive optimization, schedule adherence and prescriptive analytics.

For more information on Simcad Process Simulator, Simcad Pro Health, and SimTrack tracking and predictive analytics, please visit www.createasoft.com.

Appendix B

SUCCESSFUL SIMULATION - STEP BY STEP GUIDE

STEP 1 – DEFINE YOUR GOALS

Priority	Goal Definition	Impact on the operation	Personnel Affected
1			
2			
3			

STEP 2 – COLLECT INFORMATION

	Data to Collect	Status	Missing items and where to get them
1	Identify process flow information, general constraints, QA ratios and routing information.	• In Progress • Complete • Waiting for Information	
2	Identify cycle times, capacities and key process behavior that impact the flow.		
3	CAD Layout (if available), define distances and scaling, specific behavior		
4	Define and Add additional constraints required to complete the first goal.		

STEP 3 – BUILD AND VALIDATE THE MODEL

Steps	Model building steps	Status	Missing items
1	• Build the basic minimum constraints process flow • Identify Objects/Entities and their relationships • Validate before next step	• In Progress • Validated	
2	Add cycle times, capacities and distances. Validate before next step.		
3	Add specific routing information, QA ratios, Validate before next step.		
4	Add additional constraints required for 1st goal analysis. Validate before next step.		
5	Identify model metrics required to analyze and validate the model.		
6	Present the model to stake holders. Identify that the flow is correct and that they can relate to the model representation		

Step 4 – Overall model validation

Steps	Validation Step	Status	Missing items
1	• Collect historical data if available • Collect and compute distributions • Add/modify model metrics in order required for validation.	• In Progress • Complete	
2	Insert data in the model and perform model validation cycle.		
3	Determine if the model is conforming model. If not, Monte Carlo simulation needs to be made to validate and analyze each change going forward.		
4	Present model validation to stake holders. Everyone must agree that the model represents the environment to be analyzed.		

Step 5 – Analysis and Optimization

Base line

Steps	Base line development	Status	Missing items
1	• Initial model run – Determine the base line for the model.	• In Progress • Complete	
2	Present Base line data to stake holders.		

FOR EACH SCENARIO DEFINED;

Scenario	Scenario Definition	Status	Findings	Impact
1	List changes relevant to this scenario	• In Progress • Complete	Impact on the flow.	• Positive • Negative • Neutral
2				
3				
...				

Appendix C

Abbreviation	Meaning
AGV	Automatic Guided Vehicle
ASRS	Automated Storage and Retrieval System
CAD	Computer aided design
DC	Distribution Center
ED	Emergency Department
EMR	Electronic Medical Records
ERP	Enterprise Resource Planning
FEA	Finite Element Analysis
FEMA	U.S. Federal Emergency Management Agency
GIGO	Garbage In – Garbage Out
GPS	Global Positioning Systems
HL7	Health-Level 7
LIFO	Last in, first out
LOS	Length of Stay
MHE	Material Handling Equipment

Abbreviation	Meaning
MTBF	Mean Time Between Failure
MTTR	Mean Time to Repair
NSF	National Science Foundation
OEE	Overall equipment effectiveness
OR	Operating room
PLC	Programmable Logic Controller
QA	Quality Assurance
RFID	Radio Frequency Identifier
ROI	Return on Investment
RTLS	Real Time Location System
SAP	Systems, Applications and Products
STV	Single Track Vehicle
UCF	University of Florida
VAT	Value Added Time
VSM	Value Stream Map
WCS	Warehouse Control System
WIP	Work in Process or Work in Production
WMS	Warehouse Management Systems

GLOSSARY

Glossary Word	Meaning
ARIS	Online business process management community
Capacity analysis	Evaluation of a factory, production process or line, or machine, to determine its maximum output rate
Higher-ups	Management, C-Levels and stakeholders
Kaizen	Slow, steady progress and continual change to create constant improvement
Kanban	An automatic replenishment strategy in order to keep inventory at desired levels
Non-VAT	Time dedicated to work that does not make the entity any more valuable from a customer's perspective.
Outlier	A person detached from the main system
TAKT time	The rate at which a finished product needs to be completed in order to meet customer demand.
VAT	The amount of time in a process that is dedicated to adding value to the entity from a customer's perspective.

Simcad Process Simulator	CreateASoft, Inc. product Interactive Dynamic Simulation Software. https://www.createasoft.com
Eaches	Warehouse term for single items
SimTrack	CreateASoft, Inc. product Tracking, Predictive, and Prescriptive Analytics https://www.createasoft.com

www.ingramcontent.com/pod-product-compliance
Lightning Source LLC
Chambersburg PA
CBHW061140220326
41599CB00025B/4308